Covenant Theology

PATRICK ABENDROTH

PACTUM PUBLISHING

Published by Pactum Publishing
7940 State Street
Omaha, NE 68122

Cover Design: Erin Pille

ISBN: 978-0-9760804-2-8
Library of Congress Control Number: 202390566

DEDICATION

To all who will effectually come to embrace the glorious biblical reality that is covenant theology.

CONTENTS

Acknowledgments		vii
Preface		ix
Introduction		1
Chapter 1	What is a Covenant?	19
Chapter 2	The Covenant of Redemption	33
Chapter 3	The Covenant of Works	59
Chapter 4	The Covenant of Grace	105
Chapter 5	Covenant Theology for the Church	121
Appendix 1	The Problem of Biblicism	133
Appendix 2	Imputation, Justification, and the Active Obedience of Christ	147
Bibliography		175
About the Author		189

ACKNOWLEDGMENTS

A project like this could not be completed apart from the vital support of others. I want to thank the members of Omaha Bible Church for supporting my work in countless ways. The partnership we share in holding forth the word of truth is a delight. I am particularly grateful for the encouragement and support of my fellow elders: Frank Barber, Dallas Focht, Mike Grimes, Dave Guthrie, Mike Holloway, Chris Peterson, and Todd Swift. You men have been an immeasurable means of grace to me in so many ways.

Throughout my work on this project, the guidance, suggestions, and encouragement from Dr. J. V. Fesko have proven to be of exceptional value. Thank you, Dr. Fesko for your oversight. Gratitude is also offered to Dr. Aaron Denlinger who was the reader for this project.

Thank you to my wife, Molly, and children, Jonathan, Natalie, Alexandra, Josiah, and Owen. I am thankful for your love, prayer, and patience. My prayer for each of you, my children, is that you know and enjoy the covenant faithfulness of the Lord Jesus Christ.

PREFACE

There are those things that you cannot unsee once you have seen them. Covenant theology is wonderfully that way for me. Once I was convinced of the expressly biblical nature of the theological realities known as the covenant of redemption, the covenant of works, and the covenant of grace, the whole Bible made so much more sense and my perspective has been forever changed.

I am aware that not everyone shares my love for covenant theology. I was once there myself. At first, I was simply ignorant of covenant theology. I was not raised in a Christian home and was not taught the Bible. By God's grace I not only heard the gospel and trusted in Christ, but I was also called by God to pastoral ministry and seminary trained. During my time as a student, I was exposed to covenant theology where it got mixed reviews. Some of my professors affirmed covenant theology and others warned against it.

The initial catalyst for sorting out the issues and concluding that covenant theology is biblical and vital was the ever so important gospel matter of justification. I lived through the Evangelicals and Catholics Together (ECT) controversy in 1994 where men like R.C. Sproul and John MacArthur confronted evangelicals like Charles Colson for compromising the doctrine of justification through faith alone in Christ alone. This lit a fire in me to better understand issues related to justification leading me to read everything I could get my hands on. I was not aware of it at the time, but the historic champions of the doctrine of justification through faith alone in the finished work of Christ alone were the covenantalists.

The next catalyst drawing me toward covenant theology was the imputation of the active obedience of Christ as the basis for justification through faith alone in Christ alone. In 2012 my alma mater was embroiled in a behind the scenes controversy with one of its young professors denying the active obedience of Christ. The professor was undermining justification through faith alone by teaching that the righteousness imputed to the believer was not the perfect obedience of Christ (as taught in covenant theology), but the imputation of the divine attribute (as taught by heretics of old and opposed by people like John Owen). Making matters worse, he was being affirmed by senior faculty members. The controversy drove me to further research into matters relating to imputation and the active obedience of Christ as it relates to justification. My deep dive exploration left me more convinced than ever that Christ's active obedience is absolutely vital to justification and that covenant theology is therefore patently biblical.

In short, my path to embracing classic covenant theology has been through the doctrine upon which the church stands or falls, the doctrine of justification *sola fide* (through faith alone). Classic covenant theology teaches that sinners are justified by faith alone in Jesus alone because He perfectly obeyed the divine law and thereby fulfilled the obligation known as the covenant of works so that all who experience salvation do so by grace alone and all of this according to the predetermined purpose of the triune God before the foundation of the world as per Ephesians 1.

Covenant theology is therefore about the saving work of Jesus for sinners. It is *not* about a certain millennial perspective, baptismal views, or whether or not Israel has a future as sometimes advertised. Covenant theology is a gospel issue and therefore it is a matter of first importance.

What follows is an articulation of the manifestly biblical nature of covenant theology. As such, the covenants of works, grace, and redemption will be substantiated from the text of Scripture itself. Far from being the boogieman warned of by its foes, it is proven to be the biblical perspective of the ages that is once seen to never be unseen by the saints for the good of Christ's church and for the glory of His name.

This book is a reformatted version of my dissertation and while I accept responsibility for all errors, the project could not have been done without the influence of my professors. These include J.V. Fesko, Sinclair Ferguson, Michael Horton, R.C. Sproul, Dennis Johnson, D.A. Carson, and Derek Thomas.

Patrick Abendroth
Omaha, Nebraska
April 1, 2023

LIGONIER ACADEMY OF BIBLICAL & THEOLOGICAL STUDIES

COVENANT THEOLOGY FOR THE UNINFORMED, UNSYMPATHETIC, AND MISINFORMED

A MAJOR PROJECT SUBMITTED TO:

THE FACULTY OF LIGONIER ACADEMYOF BIBLICAL
& THEOLOGICAL STUDIES
IN CANDIDACY FOR THE DEGREE OF
DOCTOR OF MINISTRY

BY
PATRICK J. ABENDROTH

OMAHA, NEBRASKA
MAY 2016

APPROVED:

ADVISER

READER

DEAN

INTRODUCTION

Covenant theology is a coherent perspective from which countless millions of believers both young and old have understood the revelation of God in general and the all-important work of Christ in particular. For centuries it has benefited the church in this way and continues to do so even this very day. Despite enjoying such a formidable history of helping people to know God and most notably his son Jesus, many today are unfamiliar with Covenant Theology and still others antagonistically shun it.

This writer was first introduced to Covenant Theology while working on a Master of Divinity degree at which time some of his professors upheld the theological covenants of Covenant Theology as biblical and vital for a proper understanding of God, sin, and salvation. From classroom lectures to assigned texts, Covenant Theology was promoted and defended. Other professors however, vehemently warned against Covenant Theology as woefully unbiblical and extremely dangerous. This project comes some twenty years later out of the settled conviction that traditional Covenant Theology not only reflects the most accurate way of understanding the Bible, but that it is most helpful and direly needed in the life of the church from pulpit to pew.

Many have written on Covenant Theology. Wonderful works, long and short, old and new, are readily accessible. The intent of this project is not to offer something essentially different. But it is to offer something geared toward evangelicals who are either unaware of Covenant Theology and its benefits or who are antagonistic toward it.

This project will argue for the legitimacy and usefulness of historic Reformed Protestant Covenant Theology. By traditional Covenant Theology, this writer means that the covenant of works, grace, and redemption provide the framework for understanding God, his word, and his ways.[1] It will be argued that each of these three covenants are the product of divine intention and therefore are to be discovered from a normal reading of the Bible. Therefore significant attention will be given to those biblical passages teaching or supporting the covenants of Covenant Theology. Complementing the biblical support will be theologians from the past and present. Opponents will likewise be engaged at pertinent points in the discussion throughout. The vital usefulness of Covenant Theology will be a matter for each chapter with particular attention given in the concluding chapter entitled "Covenant Theology for the Church."

The remainder of this introduction will consider the significance of theology, covenant, a preview of Covenant Theology, as well as the present need for Covenant Theology.

WHY CARE ABOUT THEOLOGY?

Theology is important because of the supreme subject matter in view—God and his ways![2] There is nothing of greater importance.

---

[1] Michael Horton, Introducing Covenant Theology (Grand Rapids: Baker, 2006), 15.
[2] According to Francis Turretin, theology in "its most proper sense" is "a system or body of doctrine concerning God and divine things revealed by him for his own glory and the salvation of men" (Francis Turretin, Institutes of Elenctic Theology, vol. 1, First Through Tenth Topics, ed. James T. Dennison Jr, trans. George Musgrave Giger, Phillipsburg, NJ: P & R Publishing, 1992), 2.

God, the one true and living God, has revealed himself. To therefore know and understand this God and his ways is an unrivaled priority. God himself brings us perspective through Jeremiah the prophet:

> Thus says the Lord: "Let not the wise man boast in his wisdom, let not the mighty man boast in his might, let not the rich man boast in his riches, but let him who boasts boast in this, that he understands and knows me, that I am the Lord who practices steadfast love, justice, and righteousness in the earth. For in these things I delight, declares the Lord" (Jer 9:23–24).[3]

The deeply personal nature of understanding God and how he works cannot be overstated. To appreciate how he relates to his creation and those made in his image is one thing, but to go further and see how he not only relates, but how he is *for* his people, moves one from theology to doxology.

WHY CARE ABOUT COVENANT?

Under consideration now are reasons for interest in the topic of covenant.

THE DATA

The raw data alone voices a deafening call for everyone to care about the theme of covenant as a covenant is a formal agreement that is essentially relational.[4] Attaching "covenant" to theology therefore means that understanding God from a certain perspective is in view. That perspective is that God is expressly covenantal in the way in which he works and relates. To say much more would be to delve into controversial territory too soon. What is beyond

[3] All Bible quotations from The English Standard Version (Wheaton: Crossway, 2001) unless otherwise noted.

[4] Defining covenant as a formal agreement that is essentially relational is preliminary and to be developed and substantiated at a later point.

controversy among Christians is that covenant is very important in the Bible and that it plays a critical role in theology.

The word "covenant" is used over 300 times in the *English Standard Version* of the Bible and is found throughout from Genesis to Revelation. So much attention is given to covenants that even a first time Bible reader would not be able to miss it.

Beyond lexical support is the covenantal sense that pervades the Bible. Recognition of this is not limited to those subscribing to Covenant Theology. As one writer who is even a critic of Covenant Theology concludes,

> Given its prominence and pervasiveness in the biblical text, no preaching programme or theological curriculum can ignore the biblical theology of covenant for very long. Indeed, even when not mentioned explicitly in the biblical text, covenant is seldom far from the surface. Some texts anticipate covenant realities, whereas others are built firmly on such a foundation. Hence one cannot faithfully expound or explain the Bible without paying particular attention to this important theological trajectory.[5]

There is virtual consensus on the vitality of the covenant theme in Scripture given the data alone.[6]

A further example of how the data reaches beyond word use is in the covenantal division separating virtually all of human history. The two biblical designations of old covenant and new covenant make this very point (e.g. Heb 8). This alone would be enough to

---

[5] Paul R. Williamson, *Sealed with an Oath: Covenant in God's Unfolding Purpose* (Downers Grove: InterVarsity Press, 2007), 33.

[6] An odd example of attempting to "do theology" while virtually ignoring the covenant themes and structures of the Bible is Millard J. Erickson, *Christian Theology*, 2nd ed. (Grand Rapids: Baker Books, 1998). The Subject Index of the 1312 page volume mentions "Covenant" once with the narrow entry of "Covenant, the, and baptism of infants and children, 1102-4" (1279). Charles C. Ryrie's *Basic Theology* (Wheaton: Victor Books, 1986) is another example where no entry is made in either his definition section or "Index of Principal Subjects." Lest this be seen as trite given the limited scope of any index, one would think that "covenant" might merit an entry in a systematic theology textbook before "foot washing" or "fossils."

indicate that while the designation "covenant" is not used in every sentence of Scripture, it need not be. It is assumed that the thoughtful reader of the Bible read through such lenses.

JESUS

It is impossible to understand the work of Christ without understanding covenants. A mere starting point to seeing this is our Lord himself and the familiar words he uses in the communion prescription:

> and when he had given thanks, he broke it, and said, "This is my body which is for you. Do this in remembrance of me." In the same way also he took the cup, after supper, saying, "This cup is the new covenant in my blood. Do this, as often as you drink it, in remembrance of me." For as often as you eat this bread and drink the cup, you proclaim the Lord's death until he comes (1 Cor 11:24–26).

From this we can conclude without overstatement that *Christianity is covenantal.* After all, the drama of redemption as witnessed in the expression of Jesus just cited is covenantal.

ASSURANCE

Assurance of salvation is likewise covenantal. This is said because the covenantal oath of Jesus (i.e. his swearing) is where assurance for the believer is found. For it is in him and his commitment. The oath taken to keep the relationship intact has been made and therefore it cannot be broken as sure as Jesus is the divine Son. "This is the new *oath* in my blood" is in effect what Jesus is promising. In addition, it is Jesus who secures and thereby assures our peace with God as he is the covenant mediator. Hebrews 12:24 declares, "and to Jesus, the mediator of a new covenant, and to the sprinkled blood that speaks a better word than the blood of Abel." Given that apart from a mediator we would not be able or willing to worship God, the worthy one, we can likewise conclude that covenant is crucial to our worship.

HOPELESS WITHOUT

Disconnection from "the covenants of promise" is equal to being "separated from Christ," "having no hope," and being "without God" according to Ephesians 2:12. One does not even need to be aware of what this means to sense the gravity of the matter. Whatever these covenants are, they are the key to hope and to being with God. Interaction with the specific passage will come later.

COMPREHENDING CONTOURS

Understanding the unity and diversity in Scripture is directly related to covenants. The Bible commands many good things. But pure obedience to such commands is out of reach for sinners. So how can one really make sense of God's consistent call for pure devotion and holiness as required for acceptance by him *as well as* the grand promises of acceptance extended to sinners? This potentially perplexing inquiry goes beyond dealing with how the Old and New Testaments relate given that both call for obedience and both speak of God's grace. Grasping covenant realities is a first step on the path toward gaining an understanding of such things.

GOD IS COVENANTAL

God is covenantal and therefore relates to his people covenantally. For example, this can be observed when he addresses his people in Exodus 6:

> Moreover, I have heard the groaning of the people of Israel whom the Egyptians hold as slaves, and I have remembered my covenant. Say therefore to the people of Israel, "I am the Lord, and I will bring you out from under the burdens of the Egyptians, and I will deliver you from slavery to them, and I will redeem you with an outstretched arm and with great acts of judgment. I will take you

> to be my people, and I will be your God, and you shall know that I am the Lord your God, who has brought you out from under the burdens of the Egyptians. I will bring you into the land that I swore to give to Abraham, to Isaac, and to Jacob. I will give it to you for a possession. I am the Lord" (Ex 6:5–8).

The positive relationship between the Lord and the people of Israel is covenantal. God says that he will remember his covenant (v.5), he being the Lord, Yahweh, the God of covenant keeping faithfulness (v.6). It is the Lord who will redeem and deliver because he is the God who swears under covenant oath (v.8). He will faithfully be their God as he has made them his people (v.7). From his name to his oath taking to his oath keeping, the Lord God relates covenantally to his people.

Furthermore, the relationship between God and his people is no less covenantal regardless of which side of the incarnation one is living on. After all, Jesus himself utilized the great covenantal designation "I AM" when he spoke of the people having or not having a relationship with God (Jn 8:58; cf. Ex 3:14).[7]

With the significance of the covenant motif in view, we turn to the particular understanding of covenant known as Covenant Theology.

WHAT IS COVENANT THEOLOGY? (A PREVIEW)

Covenant Theology is a school of Christian thought that believes God relates covenantally and therefore the divine revelation of Scripture in its entirety can and should be understood covenantally. This means that God and human beings are in a covenantal and therefore formal relationship.

Covenant Theology views this relationship through two overarching covenants. The first covenant governed the relationship

---

[7] *Theological Dictionary of the New Testament*, ed. Gerhard Kittel, Geoffrey W. Bromiley and Gerhard Friedrich, electronic ed., vol. 5, (Grand Rapids: Eerdmans, 1964-), 396.

between God and Adam who was the representative of the human race. Adam did not obey God and violated the terms of the covenant. The second covenant governs the relationship between God and the elect. This second covenant is not based upon the obedience of sinners, but is the result of the perfect work of Jesus, the "last Adam" (1 Cor 15:45). Given that all human beings are related to the first Adam and believers are related to the last, the two covenants provide the only two lenses necessary for understanding everyone's relationship with God. These two covenants have been variously named. The differing names will be discussed at a later point. For now, "covenant of works" and "covenant of grace" will suffice. In general, the two names are a matter of convenience and therefore not the important part. They are labels that can and have been used as a theological shorthand of sorts that captures what is truly important which is the biblical substance of what they represent.

In his book on Reformed Theology and the Westminster Assembly, John Leith explains that Covenant Theology in the latter part of the sixteenth century and in the seventeenth century "was elaborated in the form of two covenants."[8] As such, it "became the framework for articulating the faith."[9] This is corroborated in the Westminster Confession with its utilization of "covenant of works" and "covenant of grace" designations in its seventh chapter.[10]

Sometimes Covenant Theology goes by the name "Federal Theology." This is for good reason in light of the *representative* nature of humanity's relationship with God just discussed. Respectively, the word federal comes from the Latin word *foedus* meaning "covenant."[11] So when someone discusses the *federal* headship of

---

[8] John H. Leith, *Assembly at Westminster: Reformed Theology in the Making* (Eugene: Wipf & Stock Publishers, 2008), 91.

[9] Ibid.

[10] http://www.reformed.org/documents/index.html?mainframe=http://www.reformed.org/documents/westminster_conf_of_faith.html (accessed November 27, 2010).

[11] *Concise Oxford English Dictionary*, ed. Catherine Soanes and Angus Stevenson, electronic ed. (Oxford: Oxford University Press, 2004). See also Richard A. Muller, *Dictionary of*

Adam, they are talking about the *covenantal* headship of Adam and vice versa. Federal Theology is Covenant Theology and Covenant Theology is Federal Theology.

The covenant of redemption is the third covenant of Covenant Theology. This covenant describes the relationship of the triune God with respect to his plan of redemption, a plan devised before the foundation of the world. The covenant of redemption will also be discussed further in its own section.

Prior to moving any further, it is worth mentioning one of the challenges that arises when discussing the meaning of Covenant Theology. What exactly are we talking about when we are discussing Covenant Theology? For reasons beyond the scope of this paper, it is common to hear vastly different answers to such a question. Some answer with comments about baptism, others with comments about millennial views, and still others with things like supersessionism. One almost feels as if asking the question "what is Covenant Theology?" solicits answers of such great divergence that Covenant Theology is either objectively indefinable or subjectively whatever some want it to mean. Here is where turning to an outside source for clarity can help to sharpen the focus of the discussion. In this instance, a theological dictionary can prove advantageous. *The Evangelical Dictionary of Theology*, which has enjoyed a fair amount of acceptance as a standard reference, outlines Covenant Theology using the three covenants just mentioned—works, grace, and redemption.[12] This may be different than what someone thought it meant or was told it meant, but it is a way forward that is objective and therefore most helpful.

Latin and Greek Theological Terms: Drawn Principally from Protestant Scholastic Theology (Grand Rapids, MI: Baker, 1985), 119 and Brian J. Lee, *Johannes Cocceius and the Exegetical Roots of Federal Theology: Reformation Developments in the Interpretation of Hebrews 7–10* (Göttingen, Germany: Vandenhoeck & Ruprecht, 2009), 26.

[12] M. E. Osterhaven, "Covenant Theology," in *Evangelical Dictionary of Theology: Second Edition*, ed. Walter A. Elwell, (Grand Rapids: Baker Academic, 2001), 303.

The three covenants of Covenant Theology serve to provide perspective so that the reader can maneuver the Bible's richly diverse landscape more easily and in a manner that is consistent with the divine intention. If one is reading Leviticus, Judges, or Matthew for example, perspective can be maintained with the big picture remaining in focus. The big picture being that the triune God is unfolding his purposes, humanity stands guilty in association with Adam, and ultimate hope can only be found in the ultimate deliverer who is Jesus.

This is simply put by Derek Thomas: "Covenant Theology…serves as an organizing principle that shows how biblical history and theology form a coherent, systematic whole with a unified message from the garden of Eden to the New Jerusalem."[13]

Conversely, there are things that Covenant Theology is not. First, Covenant Theology is not a humanly devised system to be superimposed upon the Bible in an attempt to force it to mean something never intended by the divine author. In fact, God relates to everyone through one of the two Adams as Romans 5 and 1 Corinthians 15 spell out. Redemptive history fleshes this out and as the storyline of Scripture unfolds, everything can and should be viewed in light of this plan, a plan that finds its origin in eternity past according to the purposes of the triune God (Eph 1). Viewing all of Scripture through the lens of Covenant Theology is viewing it as the Apostle Paul did in the aforementioned texts. For that matter, it is how he viewed the world he himself was living in.

Second, Covenant Theology is not an eschatological perspective in the more popular sense of the term. In other words, Covenant Theology is not synonymous with a given millennial view or even whether there is a future for Israel or not. The notion that it is will be addressed in some detail at a later point when specific objections are covered. For now we underscore that Covenant Theology is

---

[13] Derek Thomas, "Covenant Theology," in *The Reformation Study Bible*, ed. R.C. Sproul, (Orlando: Reformation Trust, 2015), 2351.

fundamentally about the covenant of works, grace, and redemption. Does this mean that such covenantal perspectives do not relate to or influence one's perspective on other theological understandings? Certainly, one area of theology influences others. But to reiterate, Covenant Theology at its very basic level is not, nor is it tied to, a certain millennial view, baptism view, or whether or not there is a future for Israel. This writer will argue that Covenant Theology is a theological perspective that is convinced that the Bible is to be understood through the three lenses, which are the covenant of redemption, the covenant of works, and the covenant of grace.

THE PRESENT NEED FOR COVENANT THEOLOGY

The present need for Covenant Theology is highlighted in the sequence that follows.

HUMILITY AND COMMUNITY

Countless thousands of Christian men and women have embraced and benefitted from Covenant Theology and they have done so for hundreds and hundreds of years.

Suggesting that antiquity and vastness prove legitimacy would be mistaken. That is not the intent here. But given the fact that so many Christians (young and old, uneducated and scholar), specifically those who have stood on the shoulders of the Protestant reformers, have embraced Covenant Theology, may tell us something. At a minimum, this writer's plea is that it tells us to pay attention. What did these believers, who possessed the Holy Spirit just as we do, believe? What did they actually believe?

Should we not at least humble ourselves enough to give significant pause before suggesting that the vast majority of our theological predecessors did not adequately understand how to read the Bible, the eternal purpose of God, and the way God relates to human beings?

Some, including this author, have at times been quick to brush aside such approaches because of a mindset that says, "The only thing that matters is what the Bible declares." If this is a sincere desire to be biblical, commendation is offered. But many who have professed to be most biblical have also been shown to be anything but. Biblical arguments for traditional Covenant Theology will be offered in this paper and one could state that they will be the most important factors. However, they will not be given apart from considering the arguments made by believers who have come before and have labored earnestly to be biblical. To put things rather simply, it would seem only reasonable to consider the exegetical and theological conclusions of others who were indwelt, empowered, and gifted by the Holy Spirit and not just our own.

COVENANT COMPREHENSION

There are numerous covenants in the Bible that God establishes with humans. These have similarities and differences. In addition, there is overlap. The task of observing and understanding the similarities, differences, and relationships between covenants is necessary as well as challenging. Covenant Theology is an attempt to explain the covenants in both their similarities and differences.

BIBLE GRASP

The Lord has graciously given the Scripture to his people so that his people can follow him (Ps 119:105). But how the Scripture is read and understood can be either greatly aided or tragically misguided. When the Bible is read from a covenantal perspective the grand storyline remains intact and the details are far more likely to serve their intended purpose as supporting cast members rather than rogue competitors. When readers know that the triune God purposed in eternity past to redeem elect human beings according to the predestining work of the Father, through the substitutionary work of the Son, to be applied by the power of the Spirit (Eph 1), they are prepared to better comprehend everything that happens throughout biblical history as it supports this ultimate end.

Starting with Genesis and progressing throughout, believers can expect to see God working in a way that is moving toward the fulfillment of his plan. Far from being mere ancient history, the events can be seen as movements toward fulfillment in Christ. Jesus Himself teaches that Moses, the human author, was in fact speaking of him (Jn 5:46). Instead of looking primarily for so-called timeless truths and precious principles to live out as seen in the lives of so many supposedly virtuous Bible characters, believers can be encouraged to look to Christ whether in anticipation or fulfillment.

In order for the church and its people to be healthy, there must be an understanding of the Bible in both part and whole. This is no small task. With so many books, genres, settings, and even covenants, what is the whole about and likewise the complementary smaller parts? Covenant Theology provides the answers and a corresponding helpful guide. This is why some have referred to it as a hermeneutic.[14] Oddly enough, critics sometimes pounce upon this as if it were an admission of guilt made by those underhandedly manipulating the Bible to fit a certain theological preunderstanding. Far from it, the thoughtful covenant theologian finds the Bible itself to teach the covenants of Covenant Theology. Having found the covenants to be biblical, they then provide the lenses through which all reality is to be viewed. Covenant Theology affirms the significance of authorial intent and stresses that the *divine author* of the Bible *intends* to be understood covenantally.

---

[14] As J. I. Packer states, "What is Covenant Theology? The straightforward, if provocative answer to that question is that it is what is nowadays called a hermeneutic—that is, a way of reading the whole Bible that is itself part of the overall interpretation of the Bible that it undergirds" (J. I. Packer, "Introduction: On Covenant Theology," in Herman Witsius, *The Economy of the Covenants Between God and Man: Comprehending a Complete Body of Divinity*, vol. 1, 1822; repr., Kingsburg, CA: den Dulk Christian Foundation, 1990), np.

RELATIONSHIP WITH GOD

Covenant Theology is about relationships. This makes it important to humans as relational beings. More so, it is important to us given that our most significant relationship, the one we have with God, is covenantal. It is ironic that Covenant Theology is sometimes merely associated with the theoretical and philosophical. In fact, at its very center, Covenant Theology is relational. Consider what would happen if a class on Covenant Theology were promoted as a class on relationships. False advertising would likely be the charge even though Covenant Theology has everything to do with the most important of relationships.

If there is one thing that sinners need, it is to see the state of their relationship with God. Unbelievers need to see that their relationship is hostile given covenant violation so they can see the dire need for Jesus who is the perfect covenant mediator, the one who atoned for violations and fulfilled all necessary obligations. Believers too need to recognize the wonderful covenant accomplishments secured by Jesus the worthy one.

RELATIONSHIPS WITH OTHERS

Covenant Theology can provide the objective fuel for the "one anothers" of Scripture as it helps us to not only appreciate the representative work of Christ for oneself, but for fellow sinners as well. Instead of expecting others to deserve positive treatment before receiving it, love can be shown regardless. Other perspectives may encourage such graciousness, but Covenant Theology provides a certain logic for it. If righteousness comes by federal representation rather than through personal achievement, humility and appreciation can result. Fellow sinners can be accepted not upon their righteous achievements, but as fellow recipients of what God has provided through Jesus the covenant head.

AVOIDING NOVELTY

Covenant Theology in its developed and mature form is the product not only of biblical exegesis, biblical theology, and systematic theology, but also controversy. This is true of any mature Christian doctrine as can be illustrated in historic Christological controversies regarding the deity and humanity of Jesus. The formulation of the mature Christian doctrine of Christ is in part the product of controversy and debate as opposing sides argued over different texts, understandings of texts, and relationships of texts.

We may not be fond of controversy, but some have served us well. For they allow us to avoid many of the mistakes that were made in drawing errant conclusions that ended up being exposed through arguments. This writer is reminded of this any time he needs to state his understanding of the Trinity. The last thing this writer would do is attempt to express himself in his own words and without consulting the conclusions and articulations of those who shouldered the heavy lifting in the past.

An ironic feature of the theologically novel is a position's actual lack of newness. For while there may be many different "takes," there does not seem to actually be much new under the sun even when it comes to error. Covenant Theology is not novel. But it does come to us as the result of engaging other perspectives and answering their objections.

JUSTIFICATION SOLA FIDE

Essentially all evangelicals today give verbal adherence to the reality of justification by faith alone in the finished work of Christ alone. But what they often do not know is that the theological framework for the reality of *sola fide* is vitally and inseparably linked to Covenant Theology.[15] More will be said about this at a later time,

---

[15] It is possible to uphold *sola fide* so long as one holds the substantive principles of covenant theology, as we find in historic Lutheran theology. But a richer account requires incorporation of the biblical data concerning the doctrine of the covenants.

but for now it can at least be pointed out that the declaration of God whereby he declares sinners righteous is based upon more than nothing. Far from it, God declares sinners righteous because of the righteousness of Christ, the federal head who himself fulfilled all righteousness through his obedience during his earthly ministry. Informed opponents of Covenant Theology have a problem with this given that such is bound up in a covenantal framework of understanding the work of Christ.

One of the causes for some within the broader Reformed community such as N.T. Wright and Norman Shepherd to have abandoned justification by grace alone through faith alone in the finished work of Christ alone is a drifting away from traditional Covenant Theology.[16] The connection is unmistakable upon careful examination. It seems therefore that one of the greatest safeguards to justification is to be found in Covenant Theology. This is not to suggest that only covenant theologians understand the gospel or that it is synonymous with the gospel. But it is to say that the framework upon which the gospel stands is a covenantal framework and rejecting it, ignoring it, or being ignorant of it comes with potentially devastating consequence.

CHURCH HEALTH

The church is the pillar and support of the truth (1 Tm 3:15), which is to say that it both promotes and defends the truth, most specifically the truth regarding the work of Christ. In order to carry out this ministry, the church must grasp the truth which is covenantal truth. This has everything to do with understanding the

---

[16] Whether or not N.T. Wright should be mentioned as someone within the broader Reformed community is debatable. However, he has been a contributing author for Banner of Truth (cf. John Cheeseman et al., *The Grace of God in the Gospel,* Carlisle: Banner of Truth, 1972), a publisher identifying itself with the Westminster Confession and as "a reformed, Calvinistic, conservative evangelical publisher" (https://banneroftruth.org/us/about/our-mission/, accessed December 31, 2015). Specifics about the views of Norman Shepherd and N.T. Wright pertaining to Covenant Theology and justification will be mentioned at a later point.

difference between the covenant of works, the covenant of grace, and likewise the elective purposes of God in saving sinners.

It is no less than knowing God and in turn being able to proclaim his holy law and gospel without confusing or mixing the two. And yet how many in the church, from new member to elder, are unaware of the way God relates covenantally? How can the church and its membership be seeking to honor God if ignorance about his most fundamental ways of relating to us remains unknown?

The church is in great need of rediscovering the classic doctrines associated with traditional Covenant Theology. For her health, mission, and safety, the church needs Covenant Theology.

THE APPROACH OF THIS PROJECT

Giving the uninitiated an easily accessible presentation of Covenant Theology is a great need in this writer's opinion. But given the nature of this project and its initial readership, what is offered here is a precursor to what one would hand his or her neighbor. So while much of the work here is for the uninformed or misinformed evangelical regarding Covenant Theology, it is not so without this step of an academic project. Herein is an argument for traditional Covenant Theology geared toward evangelicals, but written in this case for the well informed as this is an academic project.

As has been said, there are many excellent treatments of Covenant Theology, both detailed and introductory. However, these offerings typically have an intended readership that is at least sympathetic to the content. The aim here is not to further disciple disciples of Covenant Theology, but complete strangers and the sort of person who basically cares little about what a given church confession or theologian says.

Personally, this writer is deeply burdened for many within his associations given that they either know next to nothing about Covenant Theology or only know misrepresented caricatures that keep them from growth, effectiveness, and the joy of clearly seeing the glory of Christ in the drama of redemption offered in Federal Theology.

Specific attention to dispensational views and objections will be given throughout. This is not because they are the target. Rather it is because of the popularity of Dispensationalism in evangelicalism and more significantly for this author, it is because many dispensationalists are not aware of the essence of Covenantalism, the affirmations of Covenantalism or aspects of it by Dispensationalists, and the central importance of Federal Theology as it pertains to vital doctrines such as imputation and justification. On the other hand, movements such as the Federal Vision receive far less attention. This is not because they do not deserve attention as relevant diversions from traditional Covenant Theology, but because by and large they are not common influences upon evangelicalism.

- 1 -

WHAT IS A COVENANT

Covenant is undeniably one of the most important ideas in the Bible. Even writers from vastly different schools of thought and theological opinion agree on the significance of covenant.[17] But the likewise important task of defining covenant is somewhat of a challenge. The challenge comes because of several factors including lack of contemporary use by the general population, breadth of biblical data, as well as a degree of diversity with definitions among theologians. Addressing these will assist in defining and understanding covenant.

The chapter will show that while contemporary use is limited, it does exist with enough regularity as to not be entirely unfamiliar. A sampling of biblical usage will demonstrate that covenants are solemn agreements. Hebrew and Greek dictionaries will reveal further complementary support. Stepping beyond the lexical, Near Eastern treaties will fill in some details. The place where the divergence in opinion is most noticeable will be among the theologians. While the majority of theologians this researcher consulted were in significant agreement, there were some exceptions. This writer will conclude that O. Palmer Robertson and

[17] Peter Gentry and Stephen Wellum, Kingdom Through Covenant: A Biblical-Theological Understanding of the Covenants (Wheaton: Crossway, 2012), 21-23.

John Murray, defining covenant as "a bond in blood" and "a sovereign administration of grace and promise" respectively, are out of step with other theologians in their interpretation of the biblical data. The conclusion of the chapter will reaffirm that a covenant is a solemn agreement.

CONTEMPORARY USE

The word covenant is seldom spoken by most Americans today outside of specific settings such as church, synagogue, or real estate. Yet it remains part of our vocabulary and culture because, while spoken infrequently, contexts where it is used are weighty ones. The word covenant is used today in things such as official documents where individuals formally agree to either do something or not do something. When purchasing a house in a given neighborhood one will commonly have to agree to the neighborhood's covenants. It is regularly understood that these covenants consist of formal agreements whereby a signature by the new homeowner demonstrates his or her willingness to agree to what is specified. Similarly, real estate contracts speak of covenants and those who are writing, reviewing, and signing such documents find covenants very important. Some businesses ask departing employees to sign non-compete covenants also known as non-compete agreements.

Another ordinary though not everyday use of the word covenant in contemporary culture is at a wedding. While not universal, it is fairly common to hear the residing official follow biblical precedent and speak of marriage as a covenant (cf. Mal 2:14).

So while the meaning of covenant in today's usage may or may not be different from the Christian Scriptures and Christian theology, we have at least established that the word is not foreign to the contemporary reader. With some familiarity of covenant because of present-day usage, we turn to covenant in the Bible and then to its meaning.

BIBLICAL TEXTS

The abundance of covenant occurrences demonstrates prominence and examining even a sampling of the contexts leads the reader toward understanding. Take for example, the following six covenantal contexts from Genesis and Exodus in moving toward the meaning of covenant.

NOAH

The first use of the word covenant in the Bible is in Genesis 6:18 where God says he will establish a covenant with Noah: "But I will establish my covenant with you, and you shall come into the ark, you, your sons, your wife, and your sons' wives with you." The reader becomes aware of the serious nature of this particular covenant in v.17 where a universal death sentence is announced to come upon all who are not a part of the covenant: "For behold, I will bring a flood of waters upon the earth to destroy all flesh in which is the breath of life under heaven. Everything that is on the earth shall die." The fact that Noah's covenant relationship with God will spare him from such divine judgment demonstrates the great blessing that the covenant affords Noah.

EVERY LIVING CREATURE

Chapter nine of Genesis brings a covenant into view that is not only with Noah, but between God and every living creature:

> Then God said to Noah and to his sons with him, "Behold, I establish my covenant with you and your offspring after you, and with every living creature that is with you, the birds, the livestock, and every beast of the earth with you, as many as came out of the ark; it is for every beast of the earth" (Gn 9:8–10).

Several features in vv.8-17 are noteworthy including the associated sign, the participants being more than two, the universality ("every living creature" vv.10,12,15,16,17; "all flesh that is on the earth" v.17), and eternal nature ("never again" vv.11(2),15; "all future generations" v.12; "everlasting covenant" v.16).

ABRAHAM

The next time we encounter the word covenant is with Abram in Genesis 15: "On that day the Lord made a covenant with Abram, saying, 'To your offspring I give this land, from the river of Egypt to the great river, the river Euphrates' " (Gn 15:18).

This covenant between God and Abram is to benefit Abram and his offspring, is initiated by God, and appears gracious. More is revealed regarding the covenant with Abram in chapter 17. There the Lord repeatedly declares that the covenant is "my covenant" (vv.2,4,7), reveals it to be "an everlasting covenant" (v.7), and demonstrates that essential to the covenant is his loyalty to those who are a part of the covenant. The expressions "to be God to you" (v.7) and "I will be their God" (v.8) support this. Similar declarations are found throughout the Bible to describe what it means to be in covenant with God (e.g. Ex 6:7, Lv 26:12, Jer 31:33, 2 Cor 6:16).

ABRAHAM AND ABIMELECH

In Genesis 21:22-34 we find Abimelech calling upon Abraham to swear as one would in a treaty. We observe from this that a formal agreement has been made between two men, one that could be called promissory.

Abimelech and Isaac likewise were in covenant together according to Genesis 26:28. The context demonstrates that the covenant involved "a sworn pact" (v.28) where they "exchanged oaths" (v.31). They also shared a covenant meal where they ate and drank (v.30).

JACOB AND LABAN

The covenant between Jacob and Laban in Genesis 31:43-54 is insightful given the different elements associated with the agreement between them. The solemn nature is seen in the swearing (v.53), the presence of a judge (v.53), and witnesses (vv.44,48,50,52). In addition, sacrifice is made (v.54) and a meal is shared (v.54).

MOSES

Following the Exodus, the Lord calls Moses on behalf of the Israelites to obey his voice and keep his covenant (Ex 19:5). The exclusivity of the relationship Israel was to have with God brings to light the formality of the covenant. Any competing covenant would be a breach of the one with the Lord and would be an expression of disloyalty. There was absolutely no room for competing covenants (Ex 23:32).

Exodus 24:3-8 indicates that the words spoken by the Lord were the rules of the covenant that were to be obeyed (v.3). These rules were written down as laws to be read and heard (vv.4,7). Shed blood associated with the covenant was indicative of the seriousness of the matter (vv.5-6). As the people verbally committed to obey, they in effect swore under oath to keep the terms of the covenant (v.7).

While there are numerous covenants beyond Genesis and Exodus such as the Davidic and New covenants, this sampling should provide sufficient data to move one toward understanding the meaning of covenant.

In an attempt to reach an inclusive definition of covenant from the sampling of texts examined above and that is broad enough to encompass the differing specifics of various covenants, the following tentative explanation is offered. A covenant is a solemn agreement. Such an agreement is between two or more parties and may be accompanied by signs and ceremonies. Swearing and oaths underline the solemnity of covenants. This is sometimes underscored by the use of blood. But simply put, a covenant is a solemn agreement.

LEXICAL OFFERINGS

The reason for waiting until this point instead of starting with raw lexical studies and dictionary definitions is that such definitions are derived primarily from actual usage within the biblical text and secondarily from other ancient texts. This is not to downplay the value of dictionary offerings as they often simplify and speed up research. It is to state the obvious and make the point that the relevant passages and contexts reveal the meaning of given words. Nevertheless, what one finds in the dictionaries only reinforces the tentative conclusions just made from the textual observations.

Progressing onward to a suggested meaning for covenant by lexicographers, attention is first turned to בְּרִית (*b*^{e}*rîṯ*). The *Dictionary of Biblical Languages With Semantic Domains* offers a rather standard explanation for the lexical data. It uses words such as treaty, agreement, pledge, and binding oath of promise.[18] Observing covenant in different kinds of relationships, the summary from *The Theological Wordbook of the Old Testament* further aids our understanding:

> Between nations: a treaty, alliance of friendship; between individuals: a pledge or agreement; with obligation between a monarch and subjects: a constitution; between God and man: a covenant accompanied by signs, sacrifices, and a solemn oath that sealed the relationship with promises of blessing for keeping the covenant and curses for breaking it.[19]

---

[18] James Swanson, *Dictionary of Biblical Languages With Semantic Domains : Hebrew (Old Testament)*, electronic ed. (Oak Harbor: Logos Research Systems, Inc., 1997).
[19] Elmer B. Smick, "282 ברה" in *Theological Wordbook of the Old Testament*, ed. R. Laird Harris, Gleason L. Archer, Jr. and Bruce K. Waltke, electronic ed. (Chicago: Moody Press, 1999), 128.

Another standard dictionary underscores the solemnity associated with covenant stating, "There is no firmer guarantee of legal security, peace or personal loyalty than the covenant."[20]

As one may expect, New Testament Greek lexical resources complement the Old Testament. The entry for διαθήκη in *Greek-English Lexicon of the New Testament: Based on Semantic Domains* reads "to make a solemn agreement involving reciprocal benefits and responsibilities—'to make a covenant, to covenant together, making of a covenant.'"[21]

There are two occurrences in the New Testament where the meaning may be different. Galatians 3:15 and Hebrews 9:16 may carry the notion of a last will and testament as the word has been used that way outside of the New Testament.

The need to further cite dictionary after dictionary is unnecessary given that there is essential agreement regarding the meaning of the Old and New Testament words for covenant.

A helpful summary of the data is offered here:

> In the OT, the Hebrew word translated "covenant" is *berit*. The term probably derives from the verb *bara*, "to bind." The noun *berit* originally denoted a binding relationship between two parties in which each pledged to perform some service for the other. The NT, following the Septuagint, uniformly uses the Greek word *diatheke* for the covenant idea, avoiding the similar term *suntheke*, which would wrongly portray a covenant as a mutual contract or alliance rather than an oath-bound promise. This does not mean that a covenant may not, in some cases, take on characteristics common to a mutual agreement or contract, but the essence of the covenant concept is clearly that of a binding pledge.[22]

---

[20] *Theological Dictionary of the New Testament*, ed. Gerhard Kittel, Geoffrey W. Bromiley and Gerhard Friedrich, electronic ed., vol. 2, (Grand Rapids: Eerdmans, 1964-), 115.

[21] Johannes P. Louw and Eugene Albert Nida, vol. 1, *Greek-English Lexicon of the New Testament: Based on Semantic Domains*, electronic ed. of the 2nd edition. (New York: United Bible Societies, 1996), 451.

[22] Steven B. Cowan, "Covenant," in *Holman Illustrated Bible Dictionary*, ed. Chad Brand,

HISTORICAL BACKGROUND AND NEAR EASTERN STUDIES

Stepping outside of the realm of ancient Israel affords insight into the covenantal idea. The *Exegetical Dictionary of the New Testament* provides more perspective in understanding vassals (lesser rulers) and suzerains (greater rulers) with the following:

> Numerous verbal analogies make it probable that the *b*^{e}*rîṯ* sayings of the OT are modeled after such vassal texts and thus define Israel's relation to God as a vassal relationship of a particular kind. Even the exhortation "to 'love God with all the heart, with all the soul, and with all the might,' seems to have its origin in the loyalty oaths of the vassal to his suzerain" (Weinfeld 269). The obligations appear to be modeled after the apodictic commandments in the instructions to servants in the Hittite kingdom concerning their obligations toward royal officials...The *b*^{e}*rîṯ* theology of the OT is based upon the idea of royal sovereignty. The king's own obligation to bestow to his servants kindness, faithfulness, protection, and care precedes the covenant obligation of his subjects.[23]

Such analysis potentially sheds light on the context within which Israel related to the Lord. It also reinforces the solemn nature of covenant oaths already observed in biblical texts. Offering further commentary on ancient Near Eastern treaties from the Hittites, Leon Morris observes that

> Especially valuable are the suzerainty treaties imposed by the great king on his vassals, for in these the terms are dictated by the superior authority. The inferior simply accepts them and agrees to perform the obligations imposed upon him. The resemblances to Yahweh's covenant with Israel are plain...But there is an

Charles Draper, Archie England et al. (Nashville: Holman Bible Publishers, 2003), 355.
[23] Horst Robert Balz and Gerhard Schneider, ed. *Exegetical Dictionary of the New Testament*, vol. 1, (Grand Rapids: Eerdmans, 1990-), 299.

important difference in that, in the covenant in the Bible, Yahweh is not simply a witness and guarantor of the covenant as are the gods in the Hittite documents. He is party to it. He actually enters into covenant relation with His people.[24]

THEOLOGICAL EXPLANATIONS

Now it is time to allow the theologians to weigh in and offer definitions of covenant. The following selection includes a variety of theologians offering explanations from minimal to the more detailed. Various quotations demonstrating general consensus, albeit with differing emphases, will be offered followed by some who diverge from the norm.

CONSENSUS

Covenants are Agreements

"It denotes properly a pact and agreement…"[25]
- Francis Turretin

"But *properly*, it signifies a mutual agreement between parties, with respect to something."[26]
- Herman Witsius

"[Covenants are] solemn and ordinary oath-bound agreements that establish God and human beings in formal relationships that entail certain obligations for both parties and certain consequences for fidelity or lack thereof."[27]
- David VanDrunen

---

[24] Leon Morris, *The Apostolic Preaching of the Cross* (Grand Rapids: Eerdmans, 1955), 69-70.
[25] Turretin, *Institutes*, vol. 1, 172.
[26] Herman Witsius, *The Economy of the Covenants Between God and Man: Comprehending a Complete Body of Divinity*, vol. 1, 1822; repr., Kingsburg, CA: den Dulk Christian Foundation, 1990), 43; emphasis in original.
[27] David VanDrunen, Divine Covenants and Moral Order: A Biblical Theology of Natural Law (Grand Rapids: Eerdmans, 2014), 80.

"An unchangeable, divinely imposed legal agreement between God and man that stipulates the conditions of their relationship."[28]
- Wayne Grudem

"An agreement involving two parties—in Scripture, between God and mankind, between mortals, or between nations. It may be either a conditional or unconditional covenant."[29]
- Walter Kaiser

"It was used of agreements between men as well as of those between God and men."[30]
- Leon Morris

"A covenant is an agreement between two parties."[31]
- Paul Enns

Covenants are Commitments

A covenant is "a solemn commitment, guaranteeing promises or obligations undertaken by one or both parties, sealed with an oath."[32]
- Paul Williamson

Covenants are Unions

"Covenant [is] an oath-based union under given stipulations and sanctions."[33]
- Michael Horton

---

[28] Wayne Grudem, Systematic Theology: An Introduction to Biblical Doctrine (Grand Rapids: Zondervan, 1994), 1238.
[29] Walter Kaiser, The Promise-Plan of God: A Biblical Theology of the Old and New Testaments (Grand Rapids: Zondervan, 2009), 400.
[30] Morris, *Apostolic Preaching,* 70.
[31] Paul Enns, *The Moody Handbook of Theology* (Chicago: Moody, 1989), 631.
[32] Paul R. Williamson, *Sealed with an Oath: Covenant in God's Unfolding Purpose* (Downers Grove: InterVarsity Press, 2007), 43.
[33] Michael S. Horton, *The Christian Faith: A Systematic Theology for Pilgrims on the Way* (Grand

Covenants are Promises

"[An] Oath-bound promise whereby one party solemnly pledges to bless or serve another party in some specified way. Sometimes the keeping of the promise depends upon the meeting of certain conditions by the party to whom the promise is made. On other occasions the promise is made unilaterally and unconditionally. The covenant concept is a central, unifying theme of Scripture, establishing and defining God's relationship to man in all ages."[34]
- Steven Cowan

Covenants are Relationships

"A relationship involving an oath-bound commitment."[35]
- Peter Gentry and Stephen Wellum

"Covenants are not merely contracts or promises. Rather, covenants are relationships under authority, with both obligations and rewards."[36]
- Michael Lawrence

Covenants are Treaties

"Biblical covenants are treaties that express a committed relationship of love and loyalty (gratitude, exclusive allegiance, obligation) between God as sovereign and his chosen people as servant."[37]
- Dennis Johnson

Rapids: Zondervan, 2011), Kindle Electronic Edition: Location 26597-26598.

[34] Cowan, "Covenant," 355.

[35] Gentry and Wellum, *Kingdom*, 132.

[36] Michael Lawrence, *Biblical Theology in the Life of the Church: A Guide for Ministry*, (Wheaton: Crossway, 2010), 31. It is questionable whether covenant itself should be defined as a relationship. Where a covenant is present there is undoubtedly a relationship and the relational emphasis should not be overlooked. But to say that covenants *are* relationships is inaccurate. Instead, covenants establish relationships as Lawrence goes on to indicate when he describes a covenant as "a bond that establishes an all-encompassing relationship" (57).

[37] Dennis E. Johnson, *Him We Proclaim: Preaching Christ from All the Scriptures* (Phillipsburg: P&R, 2009), Kindle Electronic Edition: Location 4631-4633.

Evaluating the above theological definitions is largely not difficult given the similarities among the great majority of them. For where there is solemn agreement, commitment exists, there is union, oath-bound promises are practically synonymous, and a relationship exists. This is not to suggest that there is universal tacit agreement regarding the meaning of covenant with each of the writers. But it is to suggest that there is enough agreement, with nuances and particulars aside, to lead this writer to find general support for covenant meaning *solemn agreement* and thereby complementing the previously made observations from Scripture.

DIVERGENCE

Theological quotations that really stand out as oddities are those offered by Murray, Robertson, and Archer.

Bond in Blood

O. Palmer Robertson is well known for defining covenant as "A bond-in-blood sovereignly administered."[38] But do all covenants involve blood? There is evidence for blood being commonly associated with covenants given the idiom "to cut a covenant" being one and the same with making a covenant. But insisting that blood actually be essential to a covenant seems overly limiting.[39]

The over particularity here is potentially problematic. While blood may be common to covenantal relationships, it is not always in view. Therefore it should be excluded from definition. Read the most positive light, the blood could be meant to emphasize the serious nature of covenants. Supporting the seriousness view of Robertson is Robertson himself when he defines a covenant this

---

[38] O. Palmer Robertson, *The Christ of the Covenants* (Phillipsburg: P&R Publishing, 1980), 15; emphasis added.

[39] "…the action involving covenant making employs the idiom 'to cut a covenant' (Gen 15:18, etc.), that is making a bloody sacrifice as part of the covenant ritual." Elmer B. Smick, "282 ברה" in *Theological Wordbook of the Old Testament*, ed. R. Laird Harris, Gleason L. Archer, Jr. and Bruce K. Waltke, electronic ed. (Chicago: Moody Press, 1999), 128. But this does not mean that such is the universal practice.

way: "A covenant is a bond of *life and death* sovereignly administered."[40] But given that this clarification cannot and is not always made, it would seem wise to avoid the overly narrow definition of Robertson in favor of the more common variety that can be all inclusive.

Grace and Promise

John Murray says, "A Covenant is a sovereign administration of grace and promise."[41] Upon first blush Murray sounds sound. But is grace a necessary element of covenant? This is far different from asking if *some* covenants are gracious. There is no debate whether or not God is gracious in establishing a covenant with Abraham for example. But to make grace essential to the meaning of covenant is potentially problematic. Would one really want to suggest in a marriage proposal that they would like to marry in order to give the other person something they do not deserve? Less anecdotally, the covenant between Abraham and Abimelech should be considered. The appeal by Abimelech for a covenant with Abraham is not Abraham offering something undeserved by Abimelech. Conversely Abimelech says to Abraham that it is because "I have dealt kindly with you" (Gn 21:23). Murray's definition does not match all of the data so it is better to follow the vast majority and define covenant more generally. This is relevant in later considerations of God's covenantal dealings with Adam.

Gracious Undertaking

Gleason Archer also includes grace as part of his definition of covenant. He writes, "Theologically (used of relations between God and man) it denotes a gracious undertaking entered into by God for the benefit and blessing of humanity, and specifically of those who

[40] O. Palmer Robertson, "Current Reformed Thinking On The Nature Of The Divine Covenants," The Westminster Theological Journal 40:1 (Fall 1977): 76.
[41] John Murray, *The Covenant of Grace* (Tyndale, 1954). http://www.the-highway.com/Covenant_Murray.html (accessed July 9, 2015).

by faith receive the promises and commit themselves to the obligations which this undertaking involves."[42] Like Murray, Archer makes his definition too narrow. Purposeful or not, the narrowness of the definition forcibly excludes the possibility of other agreements from being covenants.

CONCLUSION

This writer returns to the definition offered tentatively at the start—a covenant is a solemn agreement. J. I. Packer captures this in a way that offers a fitting conclusion of this consideration. Packer writes, "Covenants in Scripture are solemn agreements, negotiated or unilaterally imposed, that bind the parties to each other in permanent defined relationships, with specific promises, claims, and obligations on both sides (e.g., the marriage covenant, Mal 2:14)."[43]

The significance of a proper definition that takes the breadth of biblical data into account while avoiding elements that the Bible does not universally include will allow for a more objective consideration of the covenants to be discussed in the chapters that follow.

What we have seen in this chapter is that a covenant is a solemn agreement and involves a relationship. Examples included agreements between the human and the divine. While various theologians wordsmith definitions differently, there is notable agreement about the meaning of covenant. Demanding that grace or blood be essential to covenant seems to be unnecessary and uncalled for.

---

[42] G. L. Archer Jr., "Covenant," in *Evangelical Dictionary of Theology: Second Edition*, ed. Walter A. Elwell, (Grand Rapids, MI: Baker Academic, 2001), 299.
[43] J. I. Packer, Concise Theology: A Guide to Historic Christian Beliefs (Carol Stream: Tyndale, 2001), 87.

- 2 -

THE COVENANT OF REDEMPTION

To be shocked by the realities outlined in Ephesians 1 is an experience shared by many Christians. The setting and characters are different, but the story is the same. A Christian man or woman goes from being thankful for the work of God in bringing the gospel to them and believing in Jesus for salvation to being mentally and emotionally blown away upon learning the story behind the story! That the triune God committed in eternity past to redeem elect sinners brings believers to a place of astonishment, humility, understanding, and praise. This writer has lost track of how many times he has happily heard the personal narrative of individuals rocked by such an experience. It is often expressed in terms of being eternally glad for the simplicity of the gospel and then coming to know that the gospel is even more fantastic than had been realized.

Commenting on the sort of significance just spoken of, J. I. Packer observes that "The full reality of God and God's work are not adequately grasped till the Covenant of Redemption—the specific covenantal agreement between Father and Son on which the Covenant of Grace rests—occupies its proper place in our minds."[44]

---

[44] J. I. Packer, *An Introduction to Covenant Theology* (Fig, 2012), Kindle Electronic Edition: Location 175-176.

To know something of the triune God's covenantal agreement from eternity past to redeem elect sinners is to see far more of the full reality of God's work. This is why Packer and those like him have a burden to help others to see what theologians call "the covenant of redemption." In this treatment of the covenant of redemption the examination will unfold in eight parts. Parts one through three will cover the meaning, importance, and history of the doctrine. Part four will consider vital biblical texts that provide essential elements including covenantal language, an obedience-reward reality, covenant oaths, and covenantal address. The final three sections will address the relationship between the covenant of redemption with other covenants within covenant theology, objections, and finally, some practical implications.

MEANING

The covenant of redemption is also known as the counsel of peace or the *pactum salutis*. This formal agreement (i.e. covenant) is between the members of the triune Godhead, made before the foundation of the world, and is in order to redeem the elect.

More technically speaking, the covenant of redemption is a "...covenant entered into by the persons of the Trinity in the councils of eternity, with the Son mediating its benefits to the elect. This covenant is the basis for all of God's purposes in nature and history, and it is the foundation and efficacy of the covenant of grace."[45] There have been those who have preferred to use a different title instead of covenant of redemption, but given the prominence of the designation, it will be utilized here.

[45] Michael S. Horton, *The Christian Faith: A Systematic Theology for Pilgrims on the Way* (Grand Rapids: Zondervan, 2011), Kindle Electronic Edition: Location 26607-26609.

IMPORTANCE

The significance of the covenant of redemption cannot be overstressed. For central to everything that God does in the world is his Son, the very one sent into the world to secure the salvation of those chosen and predestined by the Father. These very ones are those who will be regenerated and sealed by the Holy Spirit. This magnificent plan is God's "plan for the fullness of time, to unite all things in him, things in heaven and things on earth" (Eph 1:10). Therefore its importance is unsurpassed.

The covenant of redemption richly informs one's understanding of the gospel by pulling back the curtain and revealing the foundational background. Herman Witsius therefore observed that the covenant "is the foundation of the whole of our salvation."[46]

As the foundation of the believer's salvation, the covenant of redemption serves as the ultimate source of assurance. "In love" the omnipotent decreeing God, "predestined us for adoption as sons through Jesus Christ, according to the purpose of his will" (Eph 1:4-5). The assurance that this brings to the believer is wonderful. Salvation in Christ is irreversible as it is wrapped up in the eternal decree of God himself.

Yet the prime importance of the covenant of redemption is not the blessed assurance that it brings to the believer. There is something far more important. The greatest aspect of the covenant, giving it primary importance, is its ultimate design. The ultimate design of the covenant is seen in the stunning refrain "to the praise of his glorious grace" (Eph 1:6), "to the praise of his glory" (v.12), and "to the praise of his glory" (v.14). The most important feature of the intra-trinitarian covenant is its ultimate design, which is to bring glory to the one and only God and therefore one and only being worthy of ultimate glory. Given that there is nothing greater

---

[46] Herman Witsius, *The Economy of the Covenants Between God and Man: Comprehending a Complete Body of Divinity*, vol. 1, 1822; repr., Kingsburg, CA: den Dulk Christian Foundation, 1990), 177.

than the glory due him, it beckons our greatest interest. Contrariwise, it anticipates assault.

HISTORY

The covenant of redemption is what one may consider a standard in theology within the tradition of the Reformation. Mark Jones captures the rather unified history here:

> Determining the origins of the *pactum salutis* has proved notoriously difficult. Muller has suggested that 'hints of the concept may be discerned in Luther'. Among Reformed theologians, the earliest occurrence appears in Johannes Oecolampadius (1482-1531), who, in his lectures on Isaiah (c. 1523), speaks of a *pactum* between the Father and the Son...Moreover, in his lectures on Hebrews, Oecolampadius suggests that the pretemporal covenant between the Father and the Son provided the foundation for the covenant of grace, the context for Christology. Following Oecolampadius, on the Continent the concept is then found in Calvin, Caspar Olevianus (1536- 1587), Gulielmus Budaeus (1468-1540), Arminius, Johannes Cloppenburg (1592-1664), Herman Witsius (1636-1708), Cocceius, and a number of other Reformed theologians. Among the British writers, the doctrine is found in Edward Fisher (*b.* 1612, *d.* c. 1656), Peter Bulkeley (1583-1659), Ames, Dickson, Owen, Thomas Brooks (1608-1680), and Patrick Gillespie (1617-1675), to name but a few. Not only did the vast majority of Reformed orthodox theologians in the seventeenth century make use of the *pactum salutis* in their theology, but Reformed divines in subsequent centuries continued to speak of an eternal intratrinitarian covenant as the foundation for the temporal covenant of grace. Thus, Witsius' argument that the covenant between the Father and the Son 'is the foundation of the whole of our salvation' seems to be fairly representative of the importance of

the *pactum salutis* among the Reformed orthodox and the necessary Christological implications arising out of this doctrine.[47]

The confessional standards within the Reformed tradition likewise offer unified support for the covenant of redemption. Substantively, these include the Belgic Confession (1561), Heidelberg Catechism (1563), the Canons of Dordt (1619), Westminster Confession of Faith (1646), and explicitly the Savoy Declaration (1658). Within the Baptist tradition, the London Baptist Confession of 1689 explicitly affirms the covenant of redemption. The earliest American expressions of Reformed theology at Princeton subscribed to the covenant (e.g. Charles Hodge and B.B. Warfield). Abraham Kuyper, Herman Bavinck, and Geerhardus Vos were among the Dutch Calvinists who likewise taught the covenant of redemption.[48] Jonathan Edwards also held to a covenant of redemption.[49]

Deviance from or defiance against the harmony of affirmation would therefore seem to stand largely outside of the Reformed spirit and tradition. Such nonconformity among those who claim allegiance to the Reformation will be examined in a later section along with those outside the Reformed camp.

WHAT THE BIBLE TEACHES

A TRIUNE PLAN

There is a trinitarian purpose to redeem an elect humanity with each member of the Godhead acting. Ephesians 1:3-14 makes this matter plain as it highlights the work of the Father, Son, and Holy Spirit in carrying out the divine purpose.

---

[47] Mark Jones, Why Heaven Kissed Earth: The Christology of the Puritan Reformed Orthodox Theologian, Thomas Goodwin (1600-1680) (Göttingen, Germany: Vandenhoeck & Ruprecht, 2010), 124-125.
[48] Ibid, 125.
[49] Stephen R. C. Nichols, *Jonathan Edwards's Bible: The Relationship of the Old and New Testaments* (Eugene, OR: Pickwick Publications, 2013), 128-129.

Berkhof refers to the complementary works of Father, Son, and Spirit in Ephesians 1 as a sort of "division of labor: the Father is the originator, the Son the executor, and the Holy Spirit the applier.[50] Getting specific with the differing albeit complementary responsibilities, Herman Bavinck states that

> It is the Father who conceives, plans, and wills the work of salvation; it is the Son who guarantees it and effectively acquires it; it is the Spirit who implements and applies it. This entire work of salvation is God's work exclusively; nothing derives from humans—it is all pure grace and undeserved favor.[51]

Bavinck adds that "Just as creation is a trinitarian work, so too re-creation was from the start a triune project."[52]

The three members of the Godhead are undeniably present and active in redemption. But is their relationship covenantal? We will now see evidence for answering in the affirmative as we observe essential elements of a covenantal relationship.

ESSENTIAL ELEMENTS

If the essential elements of a covenantal relationship are present, then concluding that there is a covenantal relationship is fitting. Charles Hodge puts this into perspective and by so doing prepares one to view the relevant biblical data:

> When one person assigns a stipulated work to another person with the promise of a reward upon the condition of the performance of that work, there is a covenant. Nothing can be plainer than that all this is true in relation to the Father and the Son. The Father gave the Son a work to do; He sent Him into the world to perform it,

---

[50] L. Berkhof, *Systematic Theology* (Grand Rapids: Eerdmans, 1938), 266.
[51] Herman Bavinck, *Reformed Dogmatics, Abridged in One Volume*, ed. John Bolt, (Grand Rapids: Baker, 2011), 402.
[52] Ibid, 398.

> and promised Him a great reward when the work was accomplished. Such is the constant representation of the Scriptures. We have, therefore, the contracting parties, the promise, and the condition. These are the essential elements of a covenant. Such being the representation of Scripture, such must be the truth to which we are bound to adhere.[53]

Is Hodge justified in his declarations regarding essential elements of a covenantal relationship within the Godhead? We will now turn to relevant biblical texts to demonstrate that he is justified in his claims. We will see the covenantal realities of decretive language, obedience and reward, as well as covenantal oaths. Neither time nor space allows for an exhaustive treatment of texts supporting the covenant of redemption as they are plentiful, but the sampling that follows is offered to demonstrate the biblical nature of the covenant of redemption.

Covenantal Language

While there is more to the argument for the biblical legitimacy of the covenant of redemption, the text of Luke 22:29 demands our attention as it underscores one of the most fundamental components of the doctrine—the covenantal relationship.

When Jesus informs the disciples that he is assigning a kingdom to them as the Father assigned it to Him, Jesus uses the decretive covenantal language of διατίθημι for the assigning: "…I *assign* to you, as my Father *assigned* to me, a kingdom" (Lk 22:29, emphasis added). Such language is used in covenantal contexts for covenantal decrees (e.g. Acts 3:25; Heb 8:10; 10:16).[54] The assignment/conferral (NIV) is formal and usage would lead us to conclude covenantal thereby

---

[53] Charles Hodge, *Systematic Theology*, vol. 2, (Oak Harbor: Logos Research Systems, Inc., 1997), 360.

[54] The Lexham Analytical Lexicon to the Greek New Testament (Logos Bible Software, 2011).

indicating the covenantal relationship between the Father and the Son.[55]

An important historical note from J. V. Fesko must be mentioned here as it provides valuable insight into the development of the doctrine we call the covenant of redemption. One of the hallmarks of the Reformation was returning to Scripture as read and understood in its original languages. Pertaining to Luke 22, the return to the Greek text instead of the Latin Vulgate led Theodore Beza to a "closer exegesis of the original Greek text…in contrast to earlier patristic and medieval interpretation of Luke 22:29."[56] Remembering that the biblical text in its original language provoked exegetical interest in the *pactum salutis* is noteworthy and will be pertinent when fielding objections at a later point. But for now let it be underscored that Jesus is explicit regarding the covenantal nature of his relationship with the Father.

Obedience and Reward Covenant Realities

Time and time again in the New Testament we see that Jesus came to fulfill given obligations. This is not only consistent with covenantal relationships, it is the unfolding of the messianic prophecies according to Isaiah.

This obedience/reward theme is a covenantal one that leads us to observe that the relationship between the Father and Son is covenantal. The messianic texts of Isaiah bring this into view as they lead up to the great fifty-third chapter. According to Isaiah, Messiah is the covenant servant who, unlike Israel before him, perfectly fulfills his assigned responsibilities. This is why Isaiah 42:1 uses the titles "my servant" and "my chosen" for the Messiah. Titles reserved for God's covenant people, Israel, are now assigned to Messiah. He

---

[55] See Robert H. Stein, *Luke* (Nashville: Broadman & Holman, 1992), where he points out that "The term "confer" (*diatithemai*) can also mean *make a covenant with* and thus brings to mind the new "covenant" (*diathēkē*) of 22:20" (550).
[56] J. V. Fesko, *The Covenant of Redemption: Origins, Development, and Reception* (Göttingen, Germany: Vandenhoeck & Ruprecht, 2016), 39.

is the one to whom the Lord says "I will give you as a covenant for the people" (v.6). Whereas Israel proved an unfaithful "servant," Jesus the "Chosen One" (Lk 9:35) will be the faithful servant and honor the will of the Lord. The climax of Jesus' covenant loyalty is found in Isaiah 53 where the servant theme continues. The "servant" (v.11; cf. 52:13) succeeds in fulfilling the will of the Lord (v.10) so that many are counted righteous (v.11) and reward comes as a result (v.12).

When the Apostle Paul describes the self-imposed humiliation of Jesus in the terms of "taking the form of a *servant*" (Phil 2:7, emphasis added), the language is more than coincidental. As in Isaiah, the Messiah is the covenant servant who fulfills the desires of the covenant Lord by being "obedient" (v.8). Upon accomplishing the Lord's purposes, the servant is rewarded in being "highly exalted" and bestowed with "the name that is above every name..." (vv.9-10).[57]

Keeping this covenant-servant emphasis in mind whereby Messiah is sent to do God's will, the numerous New Testament texts pertaining to the will of God being done by the chosen servant Son can be seen covenantally as intended. Hebrews 10 illustrates this:

> Consequently, when Christ came into the world, he said, "Sacrifices and offerings you have not desired, but a body have you prepared for me; in burnt offerings and sin offerings you have taken no pleasure. Then I said, '*Behold, I have come to do your will, O God*, as it is written of me in the scroll of the book.' " When he said above, "You have neither desired nor taken pleasure in sacrifices and offerings and burnt offerings and sin offerings" (these are offered according to the law), then he added, *"Behold, I have come to do your will."* He does away with the first in order to establish the second.

---

[57] This is contrary to some Federal Vision advocates who say that the Father exalts the Son in Philippians 2 as an act of grace. See David VanDrunen and R. Scott Clark, "The Covenant Before the Covenants," in *Covenant, Justification, and Pastoral Ministry: Essays by the Faculty of Westminster Seminary California*, ed. R. Scott Clark (Phillipsburg: P&R, 2007), 184. It is instead because of the Son's obedience. Therefore the Father highly exalted Him!

> And by that will we have been sanctified through the offering of the body of Jesus Christ once for all (Heb 10:5–10; emphasis added).

What Jesus does, He does as the one sent by the Father (1 Jn 4:9) to accomplish his will (cf. Ps 40:8 as quoted in Hb 10:7 above). Even as a child, Jesus is seen acting as the obedient one who "must be in [His] Father's house" (Lk 2:49).

Jesus, according to his own testimony, is on earth in order to do the will of the one who sent him. As John 6 records,

> For I have come down from heaven, *not to do my own will but the will of him who sent me*. And this is *the will of him who sent me*, that I should lose nothing of all that he has given me, but raise it up on the last day. For *this is the will of my Father*, that everyone who looks on the Son and believes in him should have eternal life, and I will raise him up on the last day (Jn 6:38–40; emphasis added).

The relationship between the Father and the Son is one where the Son has been commissioned to carry out the will of the Father. It is not a casual relationship where the Son has come to earth with no apparent purpose or stated work to accomplish. On the contrary, the language is formal (i.e. covenantal) where the Son has come to obediently carry out the saving will of the one who sent him, the covenant Lord. The same emphasis is seen in John 5:30 and 5:36.[58]

The high priestly prayer of Jesus is a vivid indicator of the conferral-reward relationship between the Father and the Son:

> When Jesus had spoken these words, he lifted up his eyes to heaven, and said, "Father, the hour has come; *glorify your Son* that the Son may glorify you, since *you have given him authority over all flesh*, to give

[58] Michael Horton describes the covenantal emphasis in John's gospel account as "A loadstar for reflection on the covenant of redemption…where the language of 'giving' and 'receiving' a people from the Father is explicitly mentioned (6:39; 10:29; 17:2, 6-10)" (Michael S. Horton, *Covenant and Salvation: Union with Christ* [Louisville, KY: Westminster John Knox Press, 2007]), 137.

> eternal life to all whom you have given him. And this is eternal life, that they know you the only true God, and *Jesus Christ whom you have sent.* I glorified you on earth, *having accomplished the work that you gave me to do*. And now, Father, *glorify me* in your own presence with the glory that I had with you before the world existed (Jn 17:1–5; emphasis added).

Charles Hodge offers two helpful articulations of the obedience/reward dynamic in the ministry of Jesus which matches the covenant of redemption structure. He writes, "It is plain, therefore, that Christ came to execute a work, that He was sent of the Father to fulfill a plan, or preconceived design. It is no less plain that special promises were made by the Father to the Son, suspended upon the accomplishment of the work assigned Him."[59] In another place, Hodge makes the equally significant statement:

> That there was such covenant cannot be denied if the meaning of the words be once agreed upon. It is plain from Scripture that Christ came into the world to do a certain work, on a certain condition. The promise made to Him was that a multitude whom no man can number, of the fallen race of man, should be saved. This included the promise that they should be justified, sanctified, and made partakers of eternal life. The very nature of this transaction involves the idea of vicarious substitution. It assumes that what He was to do was to be the ground of the justification, sanctification, and salvation of his people.[60]

Covenant Oaths

The writer to the Hebrews (utilizing Ps 110:4) employs covenant language when speaking of the relationship between the Father and

---

[59] Hodge, *Systematic Theology,* vol. 2, 361. In describing the high priestly prayer of Jesus in John 17, Köstenberger and Swain say, "Jesus thus grounds his prayer for glorification in what Reformed dogmatics calls the *pactum salutis*" (Andreas J. Köstenberger, Scott R. Swain, *Father, Son and Spirit: The Trinity and John's Gospel* [Downers Grove, IL: Intervarsity Press, 2008]), 169.

[60] Hodge, *Systematic Theology,* vol. 3, 157-58.

the Son: "but this one was made a priest with an oath by the one who said to him: 'The Lord has sworn and will not change his mind, 'You are a priest forever.' " This makes Jesus the guarantor of a better covenant (Heb 7:21–22). Swearing, oath taking, and guarantor are all covenant terms as even the reference to "a better covenant" shows.[61]

Whether one sees Hebrews 7 as supporting the covenant of redemption or not, the fact that the relationship between the Father and the Son is covenantal is proven. Yet it is perfectly reasonable to find support for the covenant of redemption in Hebrews 7 given that the swearing of v.21 is a quotation from Psalm 110. In Psalm 110 David himself sees that Messiah will come according to the covenantal pact between the Father and the Son. For the one who "has sworn" in v.4 is "the Lord [who] says to my Lord" (v.1). Behind the Davidic covenant and new covenant is the covenant between the Father and the Son from eternity past. It is according to this *formal agreement*, as covenant has been defined previously, that the eternal purpose is "set forth in Christ as a plan for the fullness of time, to unite all things in him" (Eph 1:9-10).[62] This is not speculative or something found in the white spaces of the Bible. On the contrary, Jesus being the covenant guarantor (or surety) fulfills the will of the covenant Lord, his Father, and does so on behalf of those he represents.

---

[61] In addition, the utilization of swearing and oaths are used in Hebrews 6:13-20 where the covenant with Abraham is in view. See Philip Edgcumbe Hughes, *A Commentary on the Epistle to the Hebrews* (Grand Rapids: Eerdmans, 1977), 266-267. In describing this "special covenant, or mutual agreement made between God and Christ," Edward Fisher concludes that "Christ entered into covenant, and became surety for man, and so became liable to man's engagements: for he that answers as a surety must pay the same sum of money that the debtor oweth" (Edward Fisher, *The Marrow of Modern Divinity* [Fearn, Scotland: Christian Focus Publications, 2009]), 64-65.

[62] Charles Hodge, *Ephesians* (Wheaton: Crossway, 1994), 30. For an example of a dispensationalist recognizing the relevance of Hebrews 7 to the covenant of redemption, see S. Lewis Johnson, "The Mysterious Counsel Chamber, or the Covenant of Redemption" (sermon, Believers Bible Chapel, Dallas, TX, no date), accessed January 2, 2016, http://sljinstitute.net/the-divine-purpose/the-mysterious-counsel-chamber-or-the-covenant-of-redemption/.

Covenantal Address

The Messiah addresses God the Father as one who is in a covenantal relationship when referring to Him as *His God* in Psalm 40:8 (as referenced by Jesus in Jn 4:34). This follows the established relational address of "I will...be your God, and you shall be my people" (Lv 26:12). Not only is there a covenantal relationship between the Father and the Son according to the covenantal language of "His God" and "your God"/"my people," Psalm 40:8 utilizes the suzerain/vassal covenantal expression of "do your will."[63]

Another messianic Psalm likewise says, "God, your God, has anointed you" (Ps 45:7) which corresponds with the anointing in Isaiah 61:1, the text Jesus reads while at the synagogue in Nazareth (Lk 4:18-19). According to Jesus, fulfillment is found in him as he is the one who has been officially sent and therefore anointed by Yahweh the covenant Lord to bring good news and thereby do his will. The verbiage describing the Messiah's work in carrying out the will of the Father is expressly covenantal as befits the covenant servant theme of Isaiah (cf. Isaiah 42 and 49). So the covenant Lord has sent his covenant servant in order to establish an everlasting covenant with his people.

Psalm 2 also utilizes covenantal language to describe the relationship between the Father and the Son. Verse 7 says, "The Lord said to me, 'You are my Son; today I have begotten you." Once again we have Yahweh, the covenant Lord, addressing his Son, the one who will be rewarded with the nations as his heritage and the ends of the earth as his possession (v.8). Such emphases are befitting of a covenantal relationship according to particulars already discussed such as a covenant Lord, covenant servant, loyalty, and reward. Furthermore, Patrick Gillespie (1617-1675) argues that

[63] See Chapter 1 for a discussion of suzerains and vassals as they relate to covenants in the ancient world.

"decree" in Psalm 2:7 has linguistic and historical precedence for being translated as "covenant."[64]

THE UNBREAKABLE CHAIN RESULTS

The fruit of the covenant of redemption can be seen in "the golden chain" as William Perkins would entitle it: "And those whom he predestined he also called, and those whom he called he also justified, and those whom he justified he also glorified" (Rom 8:30).[65] The triune God works to carry out the necessary elements of that which was agreed upon in eternity past. All those *predestined* in eternity past by the Father will in time be effectually *called* by the Holy Spirit. Each of these will be *justified* by faith in the finished work of the Son therefore guaranteeing glorification in him. The genius behind such an unthwartable salvation lies not merely in the grand working of a supreme deity, but in the Father, Son, and Spirit, *the* triune God, covenanting in eternity past to save! Indeed and therefore, absolutely nothing "will be able to separate us from the love of God in Christ Jesus our Lord" (v.39).

As with other important doctrines, the covenant of redemption is not proven with a single biblical text that serves as a "slam dunk." Yet the *pactum salutis* is proven to be a biblical doctrine upon hearing from multiple verses and passages from both Old and New Testaments.

---

[64] Patrick Gillespie, The Ark of the Covenant Opened, or, A Treatise of the Covenant of Redemption Between God and Christ, as the Foundation of the Covenant of Grace (London: Thomas Parkhurst, 1677), 11-12. For a summary of Gillespie's arguments, see J. V. Fesko The Covenant of Redemption, 51-53. Gillespie is persuasive in demonstrating the precedence for חָק ("decree") and בְּרִית ("covenant") being used interchangeably. He cites two texts from Jeremiah where each considers the same realities, but one with חָק and the other בְּרִית. Jeremiah 31:35-36 speaks of the fixed/decreed order of the moon whereas Jeremiah 33:20 addresses the same issue and says, "covenant with the night." While the meaning is essentially identical, different words are employed. Therefore Gillespie appears justified in suggesting that "decree" in Psalm 2:7 can be rendered "covenant."

[65] J.I. Packer, A Quest for Godliness: The Puritain Vision of the Christian Life (Wheaton: Crossway, 1990), 58, 155.

RELATIONSHIP TO OTHER COVENANTS

Instead of considering which covenants the covenant of redemption relates to, one may rhetorically ask what covenant it does not relate to! After all, the eternal elective purpose of the triune God relates not just to all covenants, but to "all things" (Eph 1:11).

The three theological covenants of Covenant Theology are distinguishable and importantly unique. Yet they all are also vitally related. The redemptive plan of God in the covenant of redemption assumes the breaking of the covenant of works by the first Adam, the keeping of the covenant of works by the last Adam, and the covenant of grace with its differing expressions.

"The redemption through his blood" of Ephesians 1:7 being central to God's eternal purpose, is for "the forgiveness of our trespasses." Such is to point out the obvious. What may or may not be so obvious for some is that the reality of transgression assumes that the covenantal relationship between God and the first Adam will be broken.

Sinners being "holy and blameless before him" (Eph 1:4) is the result of "the riches of his grace" (v.7), "his glorious grace" (v.6).[66] The eternal purpose of God in Christ for the elect is to relate to them graciously. He freely gives to sinners eternal life, something not just unearned by them, but the opposite of what they have earned. Condemnation is deserved and "adoption as sons" (v.5) is given. This could only come from God's gracious purpose and because of his love (v.4).

How can sinners stand "holy and blameless before him" given God's just judgments? Only because of the holiness and blamelessness of Jesus, the last Adam. For he himself is holy and blameless as our representative. He is such not because of our virtue in the least, but because of God's grace to us.

---

[66] Consult chapter 4 on the covenant of grace for rationale for why it is called a covenant.

This brings us to the covenant of works, a subject to be specifically treated in its own chapter. For now it will be observed that the covenant of works has a vital relationship to the covenant of redemption. Why must the covenant of works play a critical role in one's understanding of the covenant of redemption? It really must because in order for the covenant of redemption to be carried out, Jesus must fulfill the covenant of works. As Jonty Rhodes observes, "From Jesus' point of view, the covenant of redemption is essentially the covenant of works."[67] Berkhof concurs by saying "It was for Christ a covenant of works rather than a covenant of grace. For Him the law of the original covenant applied, namely, that eternal life could only be obtained by meeting the demands of the law."[68]

Upon seeing some of the contact points between the covenants, one is prepared to recognize the vital link between the covenant of redemption and justification. David VanDrunen and R. Scott Clark spell this out here:

> The *pactum salutis* provides an essential part of the biblical and theological context for the doctrine of active obedience and hence the doctrine of justification. When Jesus Christ earned the righteousness to be imputed to his people, he was fulfilling not only the historical covenant of works as the Second Adam (Rom 5:12-21; 1 Cor 15:45) but also the covenant he made with his Father.[69]

While the active obedience of Christ is covered in a different section of this paper, for now it can be observed that the link between the doctrines is a fundamental one. Missing this link has proven and continues to prove detrimental to the church and her perspective on the justifying work of Jesus.

---

[67] Jonty Rhodes, Raiding the Lost Ark: Recovering the Gospel of the Covenant King, (Nottingham: Inter-Varsity, 2013), 118.
[68] L. Berkhof, *Systematic Theology* (Grand Rapids: Eerdmans, 1938), 268.
[69] David VanDrunen and R. Scott Clark, "The Covenant Before the Covenants," in *Covenant, Justification, and Pastoral Ministry: Essays by the Faculty of Westminster Seminary California*, ed. R. Scott Clark (Phillipsburg: P&R, 2007), 169.

To summarize and pull together the bigger picture of how the covenant of redemption relates to the covenant of grace and the covenant of works, the following entry from the Hollman Illustrated Bible Dictionary is supportive:

> Both the covenant of works and the covenant of grace are the historical outworking of the more fundamental covenant of redemption. The covenant of grace, in which God unilaterally promises graciously to redeem fallen humanity, presupposes the failure of the covenant of works. But both of these covenants depend upon that eternal covenant made between God the Father and God the Son to redeem sinners from sin and misery. Before time began, God promised to give salvation to a sinful human race. That promise necessitated the establishment in history of the covenants of works and grace.[70]

OBJECTIONS

PREDESTINATION

For those averse to the idea of God predestining some sinners to eternal life by benefiting from the substitutionary work of Jesus as they are regenerated by the Holy Spirit, the covenant of redemption will likely be found wanting. The doctrine is part of a larger theological schema that affirms the freedom of God to exercise His sovereignty in saving as he himself desires. Rejection here likely means rejection of the covenant of redemption.[71]

We will not attempt to defend the freedom of God or refute Arminianism or like perspectives here, but one could expect objections from such theologies.

---

[70] Steven B. Cowan, "Covenant," in *Holman Illustrated Bible Dictionary*, ed. Chad Brand, Charles Draper, Archie England et al. (Nashville: Holman Bible Publishers, 2003), 358.
[71] A notable exception of someone affirming a form of the *pactum salutis* while denying a Reformed understanding of divine sovereignty as it relates to soteriology is Jacob Arminius (Witsius, *The Economy*, vol. 1), 176.

LIMITED ATONEMENT

Similar to the deterministic objection is the limited atonement one. If one's theology will not allow for God to freely choose as he sees fit and without obligation to sinners other than condemnation, the notion that the Son efficaciously redeems those given to him by his Father and who will enjoy the benefits of his work according to the sure work of the Holy Spirit, the covenant of redemption will be refused.[72]

But to refuse on such grounds requires a like abandonment of what is explicit in Ephesians 1. The triune God has a plan and it will be accomplished.

In addressing this issue from the historical vantage point of Richard Baxter objecting to John Owen, Carl Trueman observes that "If the payment is refusable, then it is necessary either that God the Father is able to break a prior compact which he has made; or one must allow that the Father and Son might be set in opposition to each other relative to salvation."[73] To this Trueman immediately replies, "Neither option seems consistent with a biblical, Trinitarian doctrine of God."[74]

William Shedd is another in a long line of examples highlighting the divine purpose as it relates to the application of the atonement and the covenant of redemption:

---

[72] For an example of one who rejects the covenant of redemption and promotes universal atonement see Robert Lightner, *The Death Christ Died: A Biblical Case for Unlimited Atonement*, revised ed., (Grand Rapids: Kregel, 1998). One can only wonder about the degree to which ardent proponents of universal redemption find Covenant Theology disagreeable precisely because it does demand particular redemption with the covenant of redemption. Such would prove to be a fascinating historical study.

[73] Carl Trueman, "Atonement and the Covenant of Redemption" in *From Heaven He Came and Sought Her: Definite Atonement in Historical, Biblical, Theological, and Pastoral Perspective*, ed. David Gibson and Jonathan Gibson (Wheaton: Crossway, 2013), 219. This volume is a contemporary and able articulation of particular redemption and one to be consulted for a defense of the doctrine.

[74] Ibid. Trueman goes on to point out the obvious which is that "...the effects of Christ's death are determined by the covenant of redemption" (220).

> The atonement and its application are parts of one covenant of redemption between the Father and Son. The sacrifice of Christ is offered with the intention that it shall actually be successful in saving human souls from death...It is most rational to suppose that in the covenant between the Father and Son, the making of an atonement was inseparably connected with the purpose to apply it: the purpose, namely, to accompany the atoning work of the Son with the regenerating work of the Holy Spirit. The divine Father in giving the divine Son as a sacrifice for sin simultaneously determined that this sacrifice should be appropriated through faith by a definite number of the human family, so that it might be said that Christ died for this number with the distinct intention that they should be personally saved by this death.[75]

BIBLICIST

Rejection of an idea because the title used for it is not used explicitly in the Bible is a biblicist response of sorts.[76] One specific argument that is basically a biblicist kind is to object to the covenant of redemption because of Zechariah 6. Some covenant theologians such as Johannes Cocceius have argued that Zechariah 6 supports the covenant of redemption (also known as "the counsel of peace" from v.13).[77] Some, such as O. Palmer Robertson, have found the exegetical proof from the text to be lacking and therefore not in support of the covenant of redemption.[78] From this, Robertson and others conclude that the absence of support from Zechariah necessitates that there is no support whatsoever.

---

[75] William G. T. Shedd, *Dogmatic Theology*, ed. Alan W. Gomes, 3rd ed. (Phillipsburg: P & R Pub., 2003), 746.

[76] Biblicism will be explored and critiqued in Appendix 1.

[77] W. J. van Asselt, *The Federal Theology of Johannes Cocceius (1603 - 1669)* (Leiden, Netherlands: Brill Academic, 2001), 229. Also see Witsius, *The Economy of the Covenants*, vol. 1, 167-169.

[78] O. Palmer Robertson, *The Christ of the Covenants* (Phillipsburg: P&R Publishing, 1980), 53-54. Robertson affirms an eternal purpose for redemption, but says that "A sense of artificiality flavors the effort to structure in covenantal terms the mysteries of God's eternal counsels" (54).

The biblical nature of the covenant of redemption resides in the presence of the elements essential to a covenantal relationship between members of the triune God and not in the presence or absence of the title "covenant of redemption," "council of peace" or a variation of it. The elements demonstrating the reality of a covenantal relationship have been highlighted already. They include the language of decree, reward for obedience common to a covenantal structure, the presence of covenantal oaths, and the covenantal address between Son and Father.

If Cocceius is found wanting in his interpretation of one text, it does not necessitate the collapse of the concept provided that biblical support be found elsewhere. Such has been the finding of those who disagree with Cocceius on this one text while affirming his overall theological conclusions. Bavinck, Berkhof, and Vos unreservedly affirm the biblical veracity of the covenant of redemption without seeing support for it in Zechariah:

> The classic text (Zech. 6:13) cited in support of this doctrine does not prove anything...[79]

The name "counsel of peace" is derived from Zech. 6:13. Cocceius and others found in this passage a reference to an agreement between the Father and the Son. This was clearly a mistake, for the words refer to the union of the kingly and priestly offices in the Messiah. The Scriptural character of the name cannot be maintained, but this, of course, does not detract from the reality of the counsel of peace.[80]

Even though the scriptural origin of the term itself vanishes, in no sense does the thing need to be denied.[81]

---

[79] Herman Bavinck, *Reformed Dogmatics: Abridged in One Volume*, ed. John Bolt (Grand Rapids: Baker, 2011), 398.
[80] L. Berkhof, *Systematic Theology* (Grand Rapids: Eerdmans, 1938), 266.
[81] Geerhardus J. Vos, *Reformed Dogmatics: Anthropology,* ed. Richard B. Gaffin Jr. (Bellingham, WA: Lexham Press, 2012-2014), n.p. Accessed digitally on 1.19.16 via Google Books.

John Murray is commonly cited for his conviction that Covenant Theology "needs recasting."[82] In this spirit, Murray says of the covenant of redemption, "I prefer some such designation as the inter-trinitarian economy of salvation."[83] This is problematic on two fronts. First, even if the word "covenant" were not utilized to describe the relationship between Father and Son (though it is in Luke 22:29), the utilization of the label "covenant of redemption" in order to capture the reality of the existence of a formal relationship would be in order.[84] Second, Murray is forced to jettison the *pactum salutius* because he has rejected a traditional definition of covenant (formal agreement) and instead says "the term 'covenant' in Scripture refers to temporal administration."[85]

When certain dispensationalists take aim at the covenant of redemption, they are swift to say there is in reality no biblical basis for such a covenant, that only something like preunderstanding is the basis, and that their rejection is due to a so-called consistent hermeneutic. Besides sounding frighteningly similar to objections made against Nicene Christianity by Arians, it misses the mark on a basic level. In order for the sure saving purpose of God (as described in texts like Romans 8 and Ephesians 1) to be a reality, of course there was agreement by the Father, the Son, and the Spirit that they would correspondingly work in electing, justifying, and calling. And for there to be such an agreement, agreement demanded by the texts just mentioned and discussed previously, is for there to be a covenant.

Neither allegorical/spiritual hermeneutics nor mischievous preunderstanding is to blame for such conclusions.[86] The covenant

---

[82] John Murray, *The Covenant of Grace: A Biblico-Theological Study* (1954). http://www.the-highway.com/Covenant_Murray.html (accessed August 21, 2015).
[83] John Murray, "The Plan of Salvation," in *Collected Writings of John Murray*, vol. 2, (Carlisle: Banner of Truth, 1977), 130.
[84] According to Murray, "it is not strictly proper to use a biblical term to designate something to which it is not applied in the Scripture itself" (Ibid), 130.
[85] Ibid. For a discussion of the meaning of covenant see chapter one of this project.
[86] Contrary to those like John F. Walvoord who declares "Covenant theology is definitely a product of theological theory rather than Biblical exposition" and "is built upon a

theologian believes that the biblical data is true and understandable which leads him or her to the conclusion that the triune God's plan for redemption is one that he formally agreed to and therefore covenanted as Father, Son, and Spirit.[87]

An appendix on biblicism has been included because it is a fairly common objection to Federal Theology and because it is fairly misunderstood within evangelicalism.[88]

LEGALISTIC

Karl Barth (1886-1968) considered the covenant of redemption legalistic, though not necessarily in the way we typically think of legalism.[89] He could not accept legal dealings or obligations among members of the Trinity. Mythology was the word he used to describe it.[90] While personal and familial emphases are commonly cited as

---

spiritualizing method of interpreting the Scriptures" (John F. Walvoord, *The Millennial Kingdom* [Grand Rapids, MI: Zondervan, 1959]), 88, 90.

[87] Returning to the observations made by J. V. Fesko, it was anything but tradition divorced from the Bible that led Reformers to see a covenantal relationship between the Father and the Son, which is essential to the covenant of redemption. Commenting on their turning to the original languages, Fesko writes: "But the Reformation impulse to return to the original biblical languages rather than rely upon the Latin Vulgate drove theologians such as Theodore Beza (1519–1605) back to Luke's Greek. Where Jerome and other translators employ the term *dispono* ("appoint"), the Greek text contains the term διατίθεμαι, which means, 'to make a covenant'...Beza dropped his exegetical observation and retranslation of Luke 22:29 and it rippled through the theological waters of the sixteenth century" (Fesko, *The Covenant of Redemption*), 39. Such explicit exegetical data is just one example that contradicts the accusation of dispensationalist Michael J. Vlach who says that the "covenants of CT [Covenant Theology] are not found or rooted in the Bible. They are the product of CT's system, but they do not arise from Scripture" (Michael J. Vlach, "New Covenant Theology Compared with Covenantalism," *The Master's Seminary Journal* 18, 1 (2007): 206.

[88] Unlike previous proponents of so-called New Covenant Theology who rejected the Covenant of Redemption with biblicist like objections (e.g. Steve Lehrer), Peter J. Gentry and Stephen J. Wellum affirm the Covenant of Redemption. See Peter Gentry and Stephen Wellum, *Kingdom Through Covenant: A Biblical-Theological Understanding of the Covenants* (Wheaton: Crossway, 2012), 59-62 and Steve Lehrer, *New Covenant Theology: Questions Answered* (n.p.: Steve Lehrer, 2006), 37-38.

[89] Karl Barth, *Church Dogmatics*, 14 vols., ed. G. W. Bromiley, T. F. Torrance (Edinburgh: T&T Clark, 2010), IV/1:58-59, 62-64.

[90] Ibid, 65. Arguing for the relational nature of Federal Theology and therefore in opposition to Barth, see Gert van den Brink, "Impetration and Application in John Owen's Theology," in *The Ashgate Research Companion to John Owen's Theology*, ed. Kelly M. Kapic and Mark Jones (Surrey: Ashgate, 2015), 65-84.

proof that the legal is therefore out of the question, the biblical data describes something that is both personal and legal. A decision between the two is a false dichotomy. Jesus is the beloved Son and as we have seen in the texts referenced above, He is sent with a duty to accomplish and he swears covenantally to carry out the will of the Father.

As this writer understands it, the argument Barth puts forth is one where grace would be threatened by a covenant of redemption.[91] According to Witsius however, the covenant of redemption not only does not compromise grace, but "is founded upon it."[92]

While Barth is not a common name among evangelical laypersons, his influence extends far and wide even when he is not given credit.[93]

TRITHEISTIC

Robert Letham considers the covenant of redemption an extreme development of Covenant Theology. He believes it has tritheistic tendencies, strong elements of subordinationism where the Holy Spirit has tended to be left out.[94] But to highlight different roles between members of the Trinity is not subordinationism. Rather it is something the Bible has been shown to do. According to Berkhof,

---

[91] Ibid.

[92] Herman Witsius, *The Economy of the Covenants Between God and Man: Comprehending a Complete Body of Divinity*, vol. 1, 1822; repr., Kingsburg, CA: den Dulk Christian Foundation, 1990), 165.

[93] Determining just who is following Barth in his rejection of Federal Theology is challenging. Thomas F. Torrance would be obvious given the association to Barth and mirrored objections (see Paul D. Molnar, *Thomas F. Torrance: Theologian of the Trinity* (Surrey: Ashgate, 1988), 181-182). J. V. Fesko avoids drawing direct connections between Barth and other notable critics of Federal Theology, but does note their similarities: "The degree to which Barth influenced others is open for debate, and it is not my intention to draw a straight line of influence between Barth and other twentieth-century critics of the *pactum*. But Barth does share several similar characteristics with three other well-known critics of the *pactum salutis*, John Murray (1898–1975), Herman Hoeksema (1886–1965), and Klaas Schilder (1890–1952)" (Fesko, *The Covenant of Redemption*), 171.

[94] Robert Letham, *The Work of Christ*, Contours of Christian Theology (Downers Grove: IVP, 1993), 52-53.

subordinationism would require subordination "*as to [the] essential being* of the one person of the Godhead to the other."[95]

If the accusation of a downplaying of the Holy Spirit initially appears to give weight to arguments against the covenant of redemption, further consideration answers the objection. Cocceius, for example, has been shown to give significant attention to the role of the Holy Spirit in the eternal pact.[96]

The observation made by Michael Horton is that "a historical case can be made that wherever the covenant of redemption remained firmly in place not only as a tacit affirmation but also as an organizing principle, a robust Trinitarian faith flourished…"[97] A further observation that offers some pushback concerning John Owen's supposed neglect of the Holy Spirit is that Owen in fact went to marked lengths to draw attention to the significance of the Spirit's role in salvation in the volume dedicated to him.[98]

NEW TESTAMENT PRIORITY

A fairly common criticism against Covenant Theology is its supposed prioritization of the New Testament over the Old Testament.[99] The charge is not specific to the covenant of redemption, but is against the perspective as a whole. This writer mentions the matter at this point however given the very clear Old Testament pattern observed in the messianic texts of Isaiah examined earlier in this chapter under the section "Obedience and Reward Reality." The covenantal structure of obedience and

---

[95] Berkhof, *Systematic Theology*, 88; emphasis in original.
[96] van den Brink, "Impetration and Application," 78. For a response to Letham's analysis of Owen, see Laurence O'Donnell, "The Holy Spirit's Role in John Owen's 'Covenant of the Mediator' Formulation: A Case Study in Reformed Orthodox Formulations of the Pactum Salutis," Puritan and Reformed Journal, 4, 1 (2012): 105-106.
[97] Michael S. Horton, *Covenant and Salvation: Union with Christ* (Louisville: Westminster John Knox Press, 2007), 132.
[98] See Volume 3 of Owen's works.
[99] See John S. Feinberg, "Systems of Discontinuity," in Continuity and Discontinuity: Perspectives on the Relationship Between the Old and New Testaments, Essays in Honor of S. Lewis Johnson, Jr., ed. John S. Feinberg (Wheaton: Crossway, 1988), 75.

reward laid out in Isaiah that leads up to Isaiah 53 does not come from importing a falsely prioritized New Testament agenda. Rather the organic development and anticipation comes to its climax there in the Old Testament prophecy itself. Rather than reading the New into the Old with a supposed agenda, the Old itself prepares the reader of the New to see that fulfillment is found in Jesus, the servant, the chosen. The covenant theologian does not need to read the themes into the text that lead to an affirmation of the covenant of redemption because the themes are already there. Going further, one cannot help but to see that Paul has just such texts in mind in Philippians 2:7-10 (also discussed previously).

PRACTICAL IMPORTANCE

ASSURANCE

What could be a greater source of assurance than knowing that the triune God who does not lie, has covenantally vowed to save? Stephen Charnock, seventeenth century puritan divine continues to bless us with a taste of the practical importance of the intra-trinitarian covenant. Charnock says,

> Fly to this covenant of redemption, as well as to the covenant of grace, since that is the foundation of this. All other considerations of Christ's death, merit, and everything stored up in Christ, can give us little hope, unless we consider this covenant, which supports all the other stones of the building. Fly to it when your souls are in heaviness. Though there may be sometimes clouds upon the face of God, yet consider those compassions in his heart, when he struck this covenant with Christ. He covenanted to bruise his own Son by his wrath, while he promised to support him by his strength, and the sounding of his bowels always kept pace with the blows of his hand. The consideration of this will encourage our faintness, silence our fears, nonplus our scruples, and settle a staggering faith. Is a believer in a storm? Here is an anchor to hold him. Is he

> sinking? Here is a bough to catch at. Is he pursued by spiritual enemies? Here is a refuge to fly to. Sin cannot so much oblige God's justice to punish, as his oath to Christ obliges him to save a repenting and believing sinner. These two covenants, that of redemption, and the other of grace, are as a Hur and Aaron to hold up the hands of a feeble faith. His love cannot die, as long as his faithfulness remains, nor his peace with the soul perish as long as the covenant with his Son endures. This covenant of redemption is to be pleaded by us, as well as the merit of Christ's death, because the merit of his death is founded upon this compact.[100]

STORYLINE

The covenant of redemption is of exceeding value to the reader of sacred Scripture. With the massive breadth of material and different covenants, those equipped with a clear grasp of this biblical doctrine will be able to observe how the various strands of the biblical storyline weave together into the cohesive structure that is the redemptive plan of God in Christ by the Spirit.

We have seen that the *pactum salutis* enjoys a rich history and that such a heritage has not been without justifiable cause. For the backbone is not supposed sacred tradition, but a normal interpretation of biblical texts, specifically though not limited to, texts revealing the covenantal relationship between the Father and the Son whereby covenantal oaths would be fulfilled. This covenantal reality has also been shown to be vital in understanding the overall purpose of God in the world throughout the ages (Eph 1:3-14). The practicality of grasping the sure purpose of God has been proven to assist believers in vitally grasping the big picture of history (biblical and otherwise) and in blessing them with the unrivaled confidence in the Lord's work for his elect.

---

[100] Stephen Charnock, *The Complete Works of Stephen Charnock*, vol. 3, (London: James Nesbit and Co., 1865), p. 390.

- 3 -

THE COVENANT OF WORKS

If there was a way to explain the storyline of the Bible in a way that is faithful to the divine author's intent and helpful to those who seek to truly understand it, such would be a welcome blessing. The covenant of works has enjoyed a prominent place in the lives of believers for many years for these very reasons. It has also comforted believers by giving them assurance that God has indeed accepted them in Christ, the Christ whose work is complete. Nevertheless, it has been questioned, misunderstood, and outright rejected. Here we will examine the meaning, significance, support, history, objections, and practical importance of what many Christians have called the covenant of works.

MEANING

The covenant of works is the divinely arranged agreement whereby God would give eternal life to Adam and those he represented if Adam obeyed. This covenantal relationship is sometimes referred to with other titles such as the covenant of life, covenant of nature, covenant of creation, edenic covenant, or law covenant.

The Hollman Illustrated Bible Dictionary provides a succinct summary:

> The biblical covenant that appears first is the Edenic covenant or covenant of works which God made with Adam in the garden of Eden (Gen. 2:15–17). Hosea 6:6–7 states plainly that this arrangement was a covenant. God promised man in his state of innocence that he would give him everlasting life on the condition of his perfect obedience. Obedience would be measured by whether he kept God's command to refrain from eating of the tree of the knowledge of good and evil. However, Adam and Eve ate the forbidden fruit, thus breaking this covenant and falling under its terrible curse: "in the day that you eat of it you shall surely die…It is important to note that the covenant of works provided no method of restoration. Since it demanded perfection, this covenant, once broken, left Adam and his posterity without hope. It is in this context that we find the inauguration of another covenant, the covenant of grace.[101]

The Westminster Confession of Faith, chapter 7, paragraph 2, explains the covenant of works lucidly under the heading "Of God's Covenant with Man" by saying that "The first covenant made with man was a covenant of works, wherein life was promised to Adam, and in him to his posterity, upon condition of perfect and personal obedience."[102]

J.I. Packer offers a more elaborative explanation of humanity's original relationship with God through Adam:

> The story that forms this backbone of the Bible has to do with man's covenant relationship with God first ruined and then restored. The original covenantal arrangement, usually called the

---

[101] Steven B. Cowan, "Covenant," in *Holman Illustrated Bible Dictionary*, ed. Chad Brand, Charles Draper, Archie England et al. (Nashville: Holman Bible Publishers, 2003), 356.
[102]http://www.reformed.org/documents/index.html?mainframe=http://www.reformed.org/documents/westminster_conf_of_faith.html (accessed November 27, 2010).

> Covenant of Works, was one whereby God undertook to prolong and augment for all subsequent humanity the happy state in which he had made the first human pair—provided that the man observed, as part of the humble obedience that was then natural to him, one prohibition, specified in the narrative as not eating a forbidden fruit. The devil, presented as a serpent, seduced Adam and Eve into disobeying, so that they fell under the penal sanctions of the Covenant of Works (loss of good, and corruption of nature).[103]

More recently, Wayne Grudem offers this complementary explanation of the original covenant:

> In the Garden of Eden, it seems quite clear that there was a legally binding set of provisions that defined the conditions of the relationship between God and man. The two parties are evident as God speaks to Adam and gives commands to him. The requirements of the relationship are clearly defined in the commands that God gave to Adam and Eve (Gen. 1:28–30; cf. 2:15) and in the direct command to Adam, "You may freely eat of every tree of the garden; but of the tree of the knowledge of good and evil you shall not eat, for in the day that you eat of it you shall die" (Gen. 2:16–17).[104]

Just before making this statement Grudem stresses the representative or federal nature of Adam before the fall in stating that "In addition, in Romans 5:12–21 Paul sees both Adam and Christ as heads of a people whom they represent, something that would be entirely consistent with the idea of Adam being in a covenant before the fall."[105]

---

[103] J.I. Packer, "Introduction: On Covenant Theology," in Herman Witsius, *The Economy of the Covenants Between God and Man: Comprehending a Complete Body of Divinity*, vol. 1, 1822; repr., Kingsburg, CA: den Dulk Christian Foundation, 1990), np.
[104] Wayne Grudem, *Systematic Theology*, (Grand Rapids: Zondervan, 1994), 516.
[105] Ibid.

So under this positive arrangement established by God, Adam represented the human race as one who was in a state of unconfirmed holiness. If he obeyed God he would lead the human race into life, if not, death. It was by Adam's representative action that humanity would live or die. Likewise, it would be in the representative action of Jesus fulfilling all righteousness (Mt 3:15) that sinners would find eternal life.

SIGNIFICANCE

The significance of the covenant of works cannot be overstated. It cannot be overstated given the connection between justification, imputation, and the divine law's requirement for righteousness. It would be difficult to demonstrate this better than R. C. Sproul has:

> At the heart of this question of justification and imputation is the rejection of what is called the covenant of works...In this work of fulfilling the covenant for us in our stead, theology speaks of the 'active obedience' of Christ...Without Christ's active obedience to the covenant of works, there is no reason for imputation, there is no ground for justification. If we take away the covenant of works, we take away the active obedience of Jesus. If we take away the active obedience of Jesus, we take away the imputation of His righteousness to us. If we take away the imputation of Christ's righteousness to us, we take away justification by faith alone. If we take away justification by faith alone, we take away the Gospel, and we are left in our sins.[106]

If Sproul's analysis is correct, the significance of the covenant of works is no less than enormous for it relates to the gospel and "there is nothing less than our salvation at stake."[107]

---

[106] R.C. Sproul, "The Covenant of Works," *Tabletalk Magazine,* October 1, 2006, http://www.ligonier.org/learn/articles/covenant-works/ (accessed November 27, 2010).
[107] Ibid.

Consider too that the covenant of works with Adam and the way one views it will necessarily influence one's view of Jesus. After all, Jesus is the second and last Adam as Paul says in 1 Corinthians 15:45 and while the differences are crucial (Rm 5:12ff), their roles as representatives are inescapably parallel. Missteps regarding the relationship between the first Adam and the divine law will necessarily lead to errant views of Jesus, the last Adam. Both Romans 5 as well as parallels between the two representative Adams will be considered more closely at a later point.

In addition to the covenant of works being related to the gospel as it pertains to the work of the last Adam and fulfilling the law, is the important matter of good works as they relate to salvation. After all, obedience to the divine law is no small thing in the Bible. When one takes the requirement of obedience to the law away from Adam in the covenant of works or with Jesus after him, good works are commonly seen as a requirement for sinners in gaining justification. Those who are uncomfortable with the covenant of works do not universally hold this, but it is common enough to highlight a connection between rejecting the required obedience in the covenant of works and somehow thinking that the obedience of sinners plays a role in their justification. The significance here is with the impossibility of sinners' obedience meriting justification.

An appendix on the imputation of Christ's righteousness has been included because of the indivisible connection between Federal Theology's covenant of works and the active obedience of Jesus as it relates to him fulfilling the law and crediting sinners with his righteousness for justification.

SUPPORT

For the covenant of works to be considered true it must be biblical. But in what sense must the covenant of works be biblical? After all, both proponents and opponents of the doctrine claim that their position is the biblical one. In an effort to demonstrate the legitimacy of the doctrine as truly biblical, we will look both narrowly at specific texts of Scripture and more broadly to corresponding texts of Scripture. From there we will consult historical theology.

HOSEA 6:7

While the book of beginnings may be the logical first place to start a discussion about what happened in the beginning, this writer is choosing to interact with Genesis 2-3 after first engaging a few equally inspired texts that describe and interpret the situation with Adam in the garden, starting with Hosea.

Hosea the prophet rebukes Israel for her spiritual whoredom as she was unfaithful to the Mosaic Covenant again and again. In Hosea 6:7 he declares "But like Adam they transgressed the covenant."

If the English Standard Version's rendering is on track (likewise the New American Standard and New International versions), then this text argues for a covenantal relationship between Adam and God, otherwise known as the covenant of works. This is not an argument by mere inference or a twice-removed extrapolation via theologizing, but an explicit reference to Adam breaking the covenant with God.

Other English translations however have translated the Hebrew text differently than "like Adam." The RSV and NRSV render it "at Adam." Yet the marginal note in these versions make what Grudem calls a "conjectural emendation" by acknowledging that "at Adam" is actually to be "like Adam" according to the Hebrew text.[108]

---

[108] Grudem, *Systematic Theology*, 516. Derek Kidner says, "there is no textual basis" for the RSV rendering "which seems to rob the verse of a powerful comparison" (Derek Kidner, *The Message of Hosea* (Downers Grove, IL: Intervarsity Press, 1981), 69).

The ESV Study Bible provides a helpful summary and response to both the "at Adam" and "like men" (KJV/NKJV) options:

> The difficulty is that there is no record of covenant breaking at a place called Adam (Josh. 3:16), and it requires a questionable taking of the preposition "like" (Hb. *ke-*) to mean "at" or "in." "There" represents the act wherein Israel was unfaithful to the covenant (cf. Hos. 5:7; 6:10). "Mankind" is another suggestion for "Adam," but that would be a vague statement with no known event indicated, and therefore it would not clarify the sentence. It is best to understand "Adam" as the name of the first man; thus Israel is like Adam, who forgot his covenant obligation to love the Lord, breaking the covenant God made with him (Gen. 2:16–17; 3:17). This also implies that there was a "covenant" relationship between God and Adam, the terms of which were defined in God's words to Adam, though the actual word "covenant" is not used in Genesis 1–3.[109]

For a more nuanced as well as detailed consideration of the differing interpretive options, Duane Garrett offers this analysis:

> To what does "Adam" refer? Candidates include the following. (1) Adam is the first man, the original sinner, and thus the model for Israel's unfaithfulness. But "there" implies that "Adam" is a place, as do the parallels "Gilead" and Shechem," and this seems to rule out this interpretation. (2) Adam is the city of that name on the Jordan river. The problem with this interpretation is that the city is mentioned only in Josh 3:16 as the place where the waters of the Jordan heaped up prior to Israel's invasion of Canaan. Otherwise, it seems to have no significance. (3) Adam should be emended to Admah, the city of the plain that perished along with Sodom and Gomorrah (Gen 19:29). Hosea does mention Admah in 11:8. Otherwise, this emendation has little to commend it since Admah

---

[109] *ESV Study Bible* (Wheaton: Crossway), online edition, http://www.esvonline.org/search/hosea+6%3A7/ (accessed November 27, 2010).

> did not break any covenant of which we know. (4) The text should be translated something like, "They have walked on my covenant like dirt." This involves several unusual interpretations of the Hebrew, so that it cannot be considered probable.
>
> We thus appear to be at an impasse. A solution is possible, however, if one takes note of the unusual language the text employs. When it says, "like Adam," the reader naturally assumes that it refers to the most famous transgressor in the Bible, the man Adam. But when it says "there," the reader's reference point shifts, and he must assume that "Adam" is a place name. Inasmuch as there were shrines throughout Israel at the time of Hosea, we need not be surprised that the town of Adam would have had a shrine, nor need we suppose that the shrine there was in any respects unusual. It appears that Hosea singled out the shrine at Adam not because of some peculiarity about the town, but because of its namesake. The prophet has made a pun on the name of the town and the name of the original transgressor. His meaning is, "Like Adam (the man) they break covenants; they are faithless to me there (in the town of Adam).[110]

This is a both/and conclusion that supports the basic argument for Hosea explicitly teaching that the first man was in covenantal relationship with Yahweh.[111]

The covenant of works does not stand or fall based solely on Hosea's words, but it is a passage that has been overlooked for some time and thanks to helpful exegetes, it is being reintroduced into the discussion.

This writer finds it ironic that some opponents of the covenant of works state with such certitude that the Bible never describes Adam's relationship with God as a covenantal relationship. B.B. Warfield

---

[110] Duane A. Garrett, *Hosea, Joel*, The New American Commentary, vol. 19A, (Nashville: Broadman & Holman Publishers, 1997), 162-63.

[111] Garrett's conclusion appears similar to Byron Curtis, "Hosea 6:7 and Covenant Breaking Like/At Adam," in *The Law Is Not of Faith: Essays on Works and Grace in the Mosaic Covenant*, ed. Bryan D. Estelle, J. V. Fesko, and David VanDrunen, (Phillipsburg: P&R, 2009), 170-209.

attributed rendering Hosea 6:7 anything other than "like Adam" as "imported from without the clause itself."[112]

ROMANS 5:12-21

The word "covenant" is not used in Romans 5. But to suggest that the mere absence of the word means that a covenantal framework is not present is unfounded. After all, the word "sin" is not used in Genesis 3. But no one in his or her right mind would conclude that there is no sin in Genesis 3.

As one can argue for sin in the garden from Genesis itself, the same can and will be done in arguing for the covenantal relationship between God and Adam. But first we will focus on the divinely inspired theological interpretation of Genesis 1-3 as it appears in Romans 5.

There are two features of Romans 5:12ff supporting the covenant of works. First, Adam's relationship to God is covenantal. If a covenant is a formal agreement and therefore relationship (as previously shown), the presence of a covenant between God and Adam is evidenced in Romans 5. Adam is not free to conduct himself however he desires, but relates to God formally as God has called for obedience. Adam's relationship with God is not one between peers where Adam is free to do whatever he desires and without consequence. He is a created being and therefore relates to his maker formally or covenantally.[113]

The covenantal nature of Adam's relationship to God explains why theologians also refer to Adam as the federal head of the human

---

[112] B. B. Warfield, "Hosea VI.7: Adam or Man? " in *Selected Shorter Writings*, vol. 1 (Phillipsburg: P&R, 1970), 128.

[113] See David VanDrunen, *Divine Covenants and Moral Order: A Biblical Theology of Natural Law* (Grand Rapids: Eerdmans, 2014), 39-94 for arguments for and against a covenantal relationship between God and human beings as something tied to their being created and more specifically, created in God's image. He concludes that "God's creation of human beings in his image and likeness was itself an act establishing a covenant, whose terms would be focused (though not substantively changed or supplemented) in the supernaturally revealed commands of Genesis 2:15-17. This covenant of creation is what Reformed theology has classically understood as the covenant of works" (86).

race (federal from the Latin *foedus* meaning covenant). It is puzzling that some who reject Covenant Theology and therefore the covenant of works nevertheless claim to affirm the federal headship of Adam and Jesus. Affirming the latter and rejecting the former is in actuality a contradiction. How can someone affirm the goodness of something while simultaneously denying it? Is it a language thing? Out of ignorance of Spanish, one could say they enjoy the taste of chicken while disdaining *pollo*, but it would be a contradiction founded in ignorance. The reality is that Federal Theology *is* Covenant Theology and the federal headship of Adam *is* the covenantal headship of Adam, something vital to and inseparable from the covenant of works. Given the biblical nature of federal headship, one can be thankful for all who affirm it even if it is in ignorance of its meaning.[114]

Second, Adam's covenantal relationship with God is one that would bring eternal life to him and those he represents if he obeyed the covenantal stipulations. This is the "works" portion of the covenant of works. Romans 5 not only brings out the condemnation for disobedience aspect, but also justification and eternal life for obedience. To highlight this, note the added emphasis:

> Therefore, as one trespass led to condemnation for all men, so *one act of righteousness leads to justification and life* for all men. For as by the one man's *disobedience* the many were made sinners, so by the one man's *obedience* the many will be made righteous…so that, as sin reigned in death, grace also might reign through *righteousness leading to eternal life* through Jesus Christ our Lord.

The righteous act of Jesus that justifies and brings life (v.18) is equal to the "obedience" that brings righteousness (v.19), which is

---

[114] Given that many who reject Covenant Theology are Dispensationalists, they can be reminded that even Dispensationalists recognize that federal is synonymous with covenantal. According to Charles Ryrie, "The word 'federal' means covenant…" (Charles Ryrie, *Basic Theology*, Moody, 1999), 224.

equal to the "righteousness leading to eternal life" (v.21). To stress the obvious, it is the "obedience" (v.19)/"righteousness" (v.21) that is "leading to eternal life" (v.21). The intended parallel between Jesus, the representative of all who would ever believe, and the first Adam, the representative of all human beings, should not be overlooked. What the first failed to do, the last did which is obey and thereby gain eternal life for his people. Jesus gained eternal life for us by his obedience just as Adam gained condemnation for us by his disobedience. The explicit parallels between type and antitype (v.14) call for understanding one in light of the other and vice versa. Therefore it is both reasonable and expected that the thoughtful reader of Romans 5 conclude that *Adam was to obey and thereby gain eternal life* both for himself and for his people. It is a covenant of works because it is a covenant of obedience. To see the requirement of obedience leading to eternal life if Adam had obeyed as the fanciful construction of Protestant Reformers or those who followed them is the resultant failure to see the typological correspondence in Romans 5 that the text itself calls for. According to Paul's inspired reasoning the first and final Adam "both operate in the sphere of performance or achievement."[115]

ROMANS 10

Righteousness is arguably the best single word summary of the universal need of humanity in relation to God. For He is a righteous judge (Ps 7:11) and therefore requires righteousness. Put negatively, His wrath is "revealed from heaven against all ungodliness and unrighteousness of men" (Rom 1:18) and given humanity's universal lack of righteousness (Rom 3:10), we are universally sunk on our own. As Paul says in Romans 2:5, "But because of your hard and impenitent heart you are storing up wrath for yourself on the day of

[115] Guy P. Waters, "Romans 10:5 and the Covenant of Works," in *The Law Is Not of Faith: Essays on Works and Grace in the Mosaic Covenant*, ed. Bryan D. Estelle, J. V. Fesko, and David VanDrunen, (Phillipsburg: P&R, 2009), 232.

wrath when God's righteous judgment will be revealed." The wonderful solution to the unrighteousness crisis plaguing humanity is the justifying work of God in Christ whereby God graciously justifies (i.e. declares the unrighteous righteous). For it is God who justifies the ungodly (Rom 4:5). This message is central to Romans with lots of the detail developed in chapters three through five. But while the Apostle's focus shifts to the matter of the Jews in chapters 9-11, he has not left the topic of righteousness and justification behind. And one text that can further inform our understanding of not only justification, but the divine requirement of righteousness for justification as it relates to both the last and first Adam is Romans 10:5. The text reads: "For Moses writes about the righteousness that is based on the law, that the person who does the commandments shall live by them."

It should be no surprise that Moses is mentioned given his association with the law and righteousness being a legal word essentially meaning adherence to the law. But what may be a surprise is the theological point being made. Paul, the preacher of the gospel of grace, both affirms and utilizes Moses' statement from Leviticus 18:5 that life comes to the person who does the commandments. How can it be that Paul, not to mention Moses, would teach that the person who obeys the law gains eternal life?

How can it be? It can be if the divine standard that has been and always will be the standard for justification must be met in order for eternal life to be gained. It can be if the two "men" of Romans 5:12ff were tasked with obeying and thereby securing life for all who they represent.[116] As it turns out, the former representative disobeyed and brought death instead of life while the latter's obedience secured life. This is a federal perspective in line with what is traditionally considered the covenant of works. Before delving into further details, addressing an objection is in order.

---

[116] See J. V. Fesko, *Justification: Understanding the Classic Reformed Doctrine* (Phillipsburg: P&R Publishing, 2008), 312-313.

It could be objected straightaway that eternal life is not in view in Romans 10:5, but temporal life.[117] But to radically understate things, we have it on good authority that eternal life is in view. Consider the Lord Jesus and his response to the man who inquired about how to gain *eternal life:*

> And behold, a lawyer stood up to put him to the test, saying, "Teacher, what shall I do to inherit eternal life?" He said to him, "What is written in the Law? How do you read it?" And he answered, "You shall love the Lord your God with all your heart and with all your soul and with all your strength and with all your mind, and your neighbor as yourself." And he said to him, "You have answered correctly; do this, and you will live" (Lk 10:25–28).

The unified consensus among Moses, Paul, and most importantly, Jesus, is that life, eternal life, is gained by adherence to the divine law. In the case of the lawyer questioning Jesus, he correctly summarizes the entire law as genuinely loving God and neighbor and Jesus unreservedly commends the man's answer. Indeed such perfect law observance is beyond the reach of every single sinner and therefore a practical impossibility, but the law is the inflexible standard and strict adherence to it is the means to eternal life. This then begs the question. Would this not then mean that eternal life is absolutely beyond everyone's reach? Yes, but with one important qualifier regarding the word "absolutely." For there have been two human beings without sin—one who never sinned and one who was without sin for a time. These two and only these

---

[117] In considering the Apostle Paul's perspective in texts such as Romans 10:5 where gaining life is discussed, Bryan Estelle remarks: "When we come to Paul's use of these terms and explore the context in which he understood the promise of life conditioned upon obedience, he clearly parsed that 'life' as 'the life of eternity' or 'the world to come" (Bryan D. Estelle, "Leviticus 18:5 and Deuteronomy 30:1-14 in Biblical Theological Development: Entitlement to Heaven Foreclosed and Proffered," in *The Law Is Not of Faith: Essays on Works and Grace in the Mosaic Covenant*, ed. Bryan D. Estelle, J. V. Fesko, and David VanDrunen, (Phillipsburg: P&R, 2009), 110.

two were in a place where obedience to the law would bring justification and life.[118]

Keeping these two "Adams" in mind as the unique ones answers the objection tied to Galatians 2:16. To protect the Galatian church from errant suggestions that obedience to the law *by sinners* was required for justification, Paul declares in Galatians 2:16 that "a person is not justified by works of the law" and that this is so "because by works of the law no one will be justified." Given the severe tenor of the letter and warning of condemnation for getting the gospel wrong, few would want to disagree with the apostolic declaration that "by works of the law no one will be justified." But Paul is speaking to and of sinners who are violators of the divine law already and could never therefore be doers of the law as they already stand guilty as breakers. This has been the case for everyone who has ever lived besides the pre-fall Adam and Jesus.

The divine law's "do this, and you will live" requirement as expressed by Jesus in Luke 10 or in Paul's "the person who does the commandments shall live by them" in Romans 10 complements Romans 5:12ff and the corresponding failure and success of the two representatives. Adam disobeyed the divine law and by his one trespass condemnation came. Jesus obeyed and secured righteousness for all who would believe.

---

118 Walter Kaiser argues that Leviticus 18:5 is not regarding eternal life (Walter C. Kaiser, "Leviticus 18:5 and Paul: Do This and You Shall Live (Eternally?)," *Journal of the Evangelical Theological Society* 15, 1 (1971): 19-28). This reader commends the contribution by Kaiser for its attempt to demonstrate that "There was no alternative route to eternal life offered in the Old Testament" (28) and that Paul criticized the Jews because "they missed the central fact of law: Christ" (26). Yet the article is oddly without reference to Jesus' utilization of Leviticus 18:5. In Luke 10:25-28 Jesus explicitly relates "do this, and you will live" to eternal life. What Kaiser appears to lack, besides interaction with Jesus' use of Leviticus 18, is an allowance for the divine law to stand *in principle* as the requirement for justification as both Jesus and Paul employ it. A notable contrast can be seen in William Hendriksen's comments on Luke 10. He writes, "The trouble is not with the divine principle that perfect obedience results in everlasting life. What, then, is wrong? Paul answers in these words, 'We know that the law is spiritual; *but I am carnal, sold under sin*' (Rom. 7:14)" William Hendriksen, *Exposition of the Gospel According to Luke* (Grand Rapids: Baker Book House, 1953), 592; emphasis in original. See also John Colquhoun, *A Treatise on the Law and the Gospel* (Morgan, PA: Soli Deo Gloria Publications, 1999), 15.

While the law in view is clearly not the Mosaic law given that it had not yet come in the time of Adam (cf. Rom 5:13), law is present. This is seen in Romans 5 with the language of "trespass" (v.15,16,17,18), "judgment" (v.16), "justification" (v.16,18), "righteousness" (v.17,18,19), "condemnation" (v.18), "disobedience" (v.19), and "obedience" (v.19). All of these words are undeniably words relating to the divine law. For that matter even the word "sin" (v.12) is a word with legal weight as John the Apostle notes in saying that "sin is lawlessness" (1 Jn 3:4).[119]

Returning to the specifics of Romans 10 affords us greater clarity and insight regarding how Jesus succeeded in what Adam failed to do, which is secure eternal life for those he represents through obedience thereby fulfilling the covenant of works.

The salvation of the Jewish people is the topic in view. As Paul says, his heart's desire is that they be "saved" (10:1). To be "saved," they will need to believe in Jesus (v.9). Why must they believe in Jesus? For lots of reasons, but according to the contextual argumentation of the Apostle Paul, they must believe in Jesus in order to be justified by God (10:10; cf. Ch.3-5).[120] To put it another way, they must believe in Jesus for righteousness because he and he alone is righteous as the one and only upholder of the divine law. The contrast between the Jews and the Gentiles demonstrates not that law was the Jewish way of gaining righteousness whereas Gentiles are saved apart from righteousness or apart from any relationship to the law. Rather it is a contrast between the Jews seeking to obey the law themselves as sinners in order to gain the righteousness needed for salvation and the Gentiles who came to believe in Jesus for the righteousness needed for salvation. Both

---

[119] Contrary to some commentators who seem to go to great lengths to say that "lawlessness" has nothing to do with the law (e.g. Colin G. Kruse, *The Letters of John* (Grand Rapids: Eerdmans, 2000), 117 and Daniel L. Akin, *1, 2, 3 John* (Nashville: Broadman & Holman, 2001), 140. For a more traditional understanding of lawlessness in 1 John, see Brooke Foss Westcott, *The Epistles of St. John: The Greek Text With Notes and Essays* (London; New York: Macmillan, 1902), 102.

[120] Leon Morris, *Romans* (Grand Rapids: Eerdmans 1988), 386.

groups had the same need for upholding the divine standard, the righteous standard of the law. But the Jews failed to see Jesus as the one who brings "righteousness to everyone who believes" (10:4).

Picking up Paul's argument in 9:30-33 we see how this unfolds: "What shall we say, then? That Gentiles who did not pursue righteousness have attained it, that is, a righteousness that is by faith; but that Israel who pursued a law that would lead to righteousness did not succeed in reaching that law." Gentiles attained righteousness "that is by faith" (v.30), faith in Christ contextually. This means that they were justified which is another way of saying they were declared to be obedient to God's law. Paul does not appear critical in v.31 of Israel's pursuit of righteousness nor should he given that it is precisely what is required.[121] He says "Israel who pursued a law that would lead to righteousness" (v.31) which is principally true. There is law that leads to righteousness. Just not for sinners! The fault comes in concluding that they themselves as sinners could succeed in truly obeying the law or as Paul says specifically "succeed in reaching that law" (v.31).

According to v.32, the failure of the Jews is not that they sought righteousness, but that they sought it through their own works rather than through faith in the work of Christ: "Why? Because they did not pursue it by faith, but as if it were based on works. They have stumbled over the stumbling stone, as it is written, 'Behold, I am laying in Zion a stone of stumbling, and a rock of offense; and whoever believes in him will not be put to shame' " (Rom 9:32-33). The source of righteousness for the unrighteous must be an external source. Therefore it must be "by faith" as it is reliance upon the one who truly is righteous. The Jews failed to see Jesus as the very one who possessed the righteousness they themselves needed. Such was

[121] As Morris observes, "Paul approved of their pursuit of the law. As he makes clear in the next verse, it was not the pursuit of the law itself but the way the Jews pursued it that he saw as wrong. Paul consistently saw the law as meant to lead people to Christ and therefore to right standing with God. Properly understood, that was its function, and it could thus be called *a law of righteousness*" (Ibid), 375; emphasis in original.

not their only failure according to vv.2-4: "For I bear them witness that they have a zeal for God, but not according to knowledge. For, being ignorant of the righteousness of God, and seeking to establish their own, they did not submit to God's righteousness. For Christ is the end of the law for righteousness to everyone who believes." Religious zeal did not make up for what was lacking in knowledge (v.2) and of all things to be ignorant of, it was "the righteousness of God" (v.3). Ignorance begetting ignorance, a denigrated view of God matched an inflated view of self and the unrighteous mistakenly sought to gain acceptance with God by their own efforts. It appears that underestimating God coincided with the tragedy of overestimating self. So then rejecting the divinely sanctioned means for sinners gaining righteousness, "they did not submit to God's righteousness" (v.3). The divinely sanctioned means is Christ who "is the end of the law for righteousness to everyone who believes" (v.4).[122]

What does it mean in v.4 for Christ to be "the end of the law for righteousness to everyone who believes"? In isolation, the statement appears nonsensical. After all, adherence to the law is necessary for righteousness given that it is "the doers of the law who are justified"/"righteous before God" (Rom 2:13). It is not that righteousness now comes to sinners divorced from the law, but that "everyone who believes" in Christ is credited with the righteousness he provides as the fulfiller of the law (Mt 5:17). It is the end of the law for righteousness because Christ's righteousness puts an end to sinners relating to God via law and has them relating to God through Christ. The standard does not change and righteousness is required. But whereas sinners once related to God as hopeless law breakers, yet still obliged to keep the divine law, through faith in Christ, they can rest in the one who upheld the law and thereby gained righteousness for all who would believe.

[122] "The basic error of Israel was misconception respecting the righteousness unto justification" (John Murray, *The Epistle to the Romans*, Grand Rapids: Eerdmans, 1965), 48.

This understanding of Romans 10 aligns with what has been traditionally labeled "the covenant of works."

GENESIS 2-3

We have already seen that the term covenant is in fact used to describe the relationship between God and Adam in Hosea, but it is worth noting once again here that a common accusation against the covenant of works is that the word covenant is not used in Genesis itself.

In addition to viewing our discussion of biblicism, a closer look at Genesis itself seems in order. Genesis is not a humanly contrived theological invention amounting to little more than a redacted theology of various authors. Instead, Genesis is the divinely inspired account of beginnings whereby God utilized Moses to pen not only Genesis, but Exodus through Deuteronomy.[123] He does so for the benefit of the people of God. So in receiving Genesis 2-3, Israel did not do so in isolation. Rather they received and read Genesis 2-3 in the greater context of what is unmistakably a covenantal structure. This becomes pertinent and striking with the use and repetition of "Lord God" throughout. Starting in 2:4 and occurring again and again, God is referred to throughout as the "Lord God," Yahweh, the *covenant* God. Some twenty times, this covenant title is used in Genesis 2-3.[124]

To therefore conclude that because Genesis 2-3 does not use the word "covenant" there is to be no covenant found, is myopic and misleading. The covenant making God is speaking throughout and is explicitly spoken of with his unambiguous title. It is therefore unthinkable to forbid any covenantal workings. Put more positively, of course Yahweh, the covenant making and covenant keeping God,

---

123 Gleason Archer, *A Survey of Old Testament Introduction* (Chicago: Moody Press, 2007).
124 2:4,5,7,8,9,15,16,18,19,21,22, 3:1,8 (2x), 9,13,14,21,22,23.

is acting and speaking covenantally in his engagement with Adam. After all, he is Yahweh![125]

As has been said elsewhere, the word "sin" is absent from Genesis 2-3, but it is most definitely what Adam does in the garden. Likewise, the Lord God spells out covenant obligations and consequences for the breaking of them.

Congruently, Adam is not to be seen as an independent being with no obligations. Instead, Adam is a created being who has heard from his creator-sovereign just what is expected of him as such and what will happen if there is violation. In other words, there is a formal relationship between Yahweh and Adam that is therefore a covenantal relationship.

Like Romans 5, the Genesis account informs our understanding of the representative nature of Adam. It was the sin of Adam that brought death to all who followed. Those who came after him were not put back into the garden to repeat the testing. Instead, they were banished. In the words of evangelical preacher Martin Lloyd-Jones,

> God originally made a covenant with Adam. You remember that He put him into the Garden and told him that if he did certain things he would have a certain reward. That is called a covenant of works, because Adam's inheritance of this promise was entirely dependent upon his works, upon what he did. But, you remember, Adam broke the covenant; he failed, and landed himself and his posterity in the terrible plight that we have been describing. So, from there on God has made a new covenant, which is called the *covenant of grace.*[126]

---

[125] VanDrunen, *Divine Covenants*, 81. Also see comments on the creator/creature relationship being covenantal in the previous section dealing with Romans 5.
[126] David Martyn Lloyd-Jones, *God the Father, God the Son* (Wheaton: Crossway Books, 1996), 226; italics in original.

ROMANS 2:13

The notion of God requiring strict and perfect adherence to his law finds further support in Romans 2:13: "For it is not the hearers of the law who are righteous before God, but the doers of the law who will be justified." As part of Paul's argument in Romans 1:18-3:20 demonstrating that no one could ever be justified on their own given that all are in actuality unrighteous, he clearly states the requirement of God the righteous judge. The requirement for being justified by God is nothing short of actually being "doers of the law" (v.13). The immediate occasion is pressing those who possessed the law and were familiar with what it said with the startling reminder that such is not enough. It is not enough to know what the law says (being a hearer), but one must be a doer to be justified.

To be certain, Paul is not stating that sinners can be justified by being doers of the law. "For by works of the law no human being will be justified!" (3:20a). But what cannot be done due to violators of the law already being violators of the law, does not detract from the standard remaining the standard. The reality and truism remains—it is "the doers of the law who will be justified." As Charles Hodge observes, "He is not speaking of the method of justification available for sinners, as revealed in the gospel, but of the principles of justice which will be applied to all who look to the law for justification."[127]

Competing alternatives for interpreting Romans 2:13 require one to either alter the straightforward wording of the text or contradict the overall Pauline argument of justification *sola fide.*

While it is true that there is to be a so-called "evangelical obedience" where those who are justified by faith alone and enjoy the wonderful things that come to those who experience God's saving grace, it seems beyond a stretch to make the words "the doers of the law who will be justified" (v.13) to even come close to saying

---

[127] Charles Hodge, *Commentary on the Epistle to the Romans* (New York: Hodder & Stoughton, 1886), 82.

that. The intent of protecting justification *sola fide* is commendable to be sure and it is true that obedience is to follow justification. But such a conclusion from Romans 2 not only discounts the actual wording of the text, it also ignores the development of the argument in Romans. For Paul is at this point in the midst of exposing *everyone* as guilty before God and therefore in need of the justifying work of Jesus. To insert a comment about Christian fruitfulness would be out of place entirely. From 1:18 through 3:20 the screws are tightened more and more to expose everyone as guilty and in need of salvation in Christ.

John Piper is an example of someone who argues for Romans 2:13 being an evangelical obedience (though not utilizing this title).[128] He says,

> I think that when Paul says, "doers of the law will be justified," he means that there really are such people, and they are the only people who will be acquitted at the judgment. This is not a hypothetical statement. It is a statement of actual, experienced fact. When Christ comes into a person's life by the power of the Holy Spirit through faith in the Gospel, that person becomes a "doer of the law." Not a sinlessly perfect law-keeper, but one who loves the law of God (= the law of Christ), and depends on God's help to live according to the truth (which now includes the cross of Christ and the work of the Spirit), and trusts God for his mercy when he stumbles (according to 1 John 1:9).[129]

---

[128] Piper appears more amicable in a later publication to something that is at least closer to more of a Reformed understanding of Romans 2:13, though still not articulating it outright. See John Piper, *The Future of Justification: A Response to N.T. Wright* (Wheaton: Crossway, 2007), 109. It is intriguing to observe the similarity between Wright and Piper on Romans 2. In a stated "clarification," Piper acknowledges that his views on justification have been "sharpened." This is offered as an explanation for why "some people have felt tensions between the first edition of *Future Grace* and the message of those books [(e.g. *The Future of Justification: A Response to N. T. Wright*)]" (John Piper, *Future Grace: The Purifying Power of the Promises of God,* revised ed., Colorado Springs: Multnomah Books, 2012), XI.

[129] John Piper, "There Is No Partiality with God, Part 2" (sermon, Bethlehem Baptist Church, Minneapolis, MN, January 31, 1999), accessed November 2, 2015, http://www.desiringgod.org/messages/there-is-no-partiality-with-god-part-2. A similar

If Piper is correct, Romans 2:13 does not offer any support for the covenant of works. But there are multiple challenges to his interpretation. First, the distance between what the verse actually says and what he says Paul means is substantial. The text says that the doers of the law will be justified. Piper essentially turns the verse on its head and makes it to mean Christians who try (albeit imperfectly, though with God's help) will be justified. The resemblance between this and a Roman Catholic view of justification is unnerving.[130]

Second, the isolation of Romans 2 from the context of the whole of 1:18-3:20 has led to an interpretation that derails Paul's argument of universal guilt with no one being righteous, "no, not one" (Rom 3:10). Piper would thankfully concur with 3:10 and avoid tinkering with its basic meaning as he affirms the universal guilt of humanity. But if one reads Romans 1:18-3:20 as a unified argument for universal guilt, John Piper has in effect created an exception and a category of persons who are righteous. He says that "Doer of the law' doesn't mean sinless perfection,"[131] but given where it occurs in Paul's argument, there is every reason to conclude that it means just that. The standard for justification is actually being righteous. All will be shown to be unrighteous and therefore outside of any hope of justification apart from the work of Christ!

---

view to Piper's can be found in Thomas R. Schreiner, *Paul, Apostle of God's Glory in Christ: A Pauline Theology* (Downers Grove, IL; Leicester, England: IVP Academic; Apollos, 2006), 281-82. In a more recent publication Schreiner argues that James 2 teaches that sinners will be justified before God by their works (Thomas R. Schreiner, *Faith Alone: The Doctrine of Justification* (Grand Rapids, MI: Zondervan, 2015), 205-206. While qualifications are offered in an attempt to demonstrate a soteriology that is not at odds with *sola fide,* the emphasis upon justification by works gives this writer cause for concern. Conelis P. Venema engages the views of Schreiner and others regarding Romans 2:13 in *The Gospel of Free Acceptance in Christ: An Assessment of the Reformation and 'New Perspectives' on Paul* (Carlisle, PA: The Banner of Truth Trust, 2006), 276-292.

130 See "Grace and Justification" in *Catechism of the Catholic Church.* http://www.vatican.va/archive/ccc_css/archive/catechism/p3s1c3a2.htm (accessed November 2, 2015).

131 Piper, "There is No Partiality."

Third, Piper defends his view by arguing that there is no conflict between Romans 2:13 and 3:20. He argues,

> Romans 2:13b says, 'Doers of the Law will be justified.' It does not say, 'By doing works of the Law you will be justified.' It simply says that the ones who will be justified are also those who are doers of the law. There is no causal connection asserted. So the verse is not a contradiction of Romans 3:20 which says, 'By the works of the Law no flesh will be justified.[132]

At this point it is very difficult to ascertain what John Piper is saying as he is seemingly saying that what Romans 2:13 says, it does not really say and therefore there is no conflict between justification being by works of the law and not being by works of the law.

Fourth, Piper's explanation of 2:13 potentially detracts from the present reality of justification. For Romans 5:1 states, "Therefore, since *we have been justified* by faith, we have peace with God through our Lord Jesus Christ" (emphasis added). This is not because we are doers of the law, but because Jesus Christ was just that for us. As sure as his work is complete our justification is also.

Despite the potential confusion found in John Piper's understanding of Romans 2:13, we can be thankful that in the same article, he says "There is coming a final day of judgment. We will all give an account of ourselves to God. Faith in Christ as our righteousness will be our only hope for acceptance with God (Romans 1:16-17; 3:20-26)."[133]

Rounding out a consideration of Romans 2:13 is this refreshingly straightforward interpretation and commentary from John Calvin:

> The import then of this verse is the following, — "That if righteousness be sought from the law, the law must be fulfilled; for the righteousness of the law consists in the perfection of works."

[132] Ibid.
[133] Ibid.

> They who pervert this passage for the purpose of building up justification by works, deserve most fully to be laughed at even by children. It is therefore improper and beyond what is needful, to introduce here a long discussion on the subject, with the view of exposing so futile a sophistry: for the Apostle only urges here on the Jews what he had mentioned, the decision of the law, — That by the law they could not be justified, except they fulfilled the law, that if they transgressed it, a curse was instantly pronounced on them. Now we do not deny but that perfect righteousness is prescribed in the law: but as all are convicted of transgression, we say that another righteousness must be sought. Still more, we can prove from this passage that no one is justified by works; for if they alone are justified by the law who fulfill the law, it follows that no one is justified; for no one can be found who can boast of having fulfilled the law.[134]

Returning to the interface between such discussions of the law and the covenant of works, we find that one of two things happens. We see that God requires absolute adherence to his law for justification and therefore the need for obedience to the law. This then compels some to find sinners cooperating with grace and being justified (an actual impossibility) or others to uphold the classic reformation doctrine of *sola fide* and its corresponding covenant of works whereby Jesus' perfect obedience to the law brings the reality of an imputed righteousness and justification.

---

[134] John Calvin, *Commentary on Romans* (Christian Classics Ethereal Library). http://www.ccel.org/ccel/calvin/calcom38.vi.iii.html (accessed November 2, 2015). It is worth observing how Calvin utilizes Romans 2:13 in much the same way as those who come after him do in articulating the covenant of works. The point being that while doctrinal development occurred, the same general theological perspective was shared regarding the federal headship of Adam. In other words, Calvin and the Westminster Confession of Faith were not at odds. See Richard A. Muller, *Calvin and the Reformed Tradition: On the Work of Christ and the Order of Salvation* (Grand Rapids: Baker Academic, 2012) where Muller challenges supposed "Calvin verses the Calvinists" perspectives as being without legitimate warrant.

HISTORY AND PROPONENTS

Before naming historical figures who affirmed the covenant of works, a couple of observations will be offered. First, it is acknowledged that antiquity is not synonymous with orthodoxy. In other words, this writer acknowledges that the truthfulness of a doctrine or lack thereof does not rest on it being old. After all, heresies are flourishing even in the first century as Galatians corroborates. Truthfulness must reside in the biblical nature of something. With the priority given to the text of Scripture, it is now and only now that we turn to history.

Given that we are not the first Christians, one should expect to be able to learn about Christianity from those who have gone before us. Believers before us had the Scripture, the Holy Spirit, as well as controversies that often forced them to carefully draw upon the Scripture both narrowly and broadly in order to formulate theological conclusions and thereby fight the good fight for the faith that had been once and for all entrusted to the saints (Jude 3-4). Where this has happened, believers utilize the formulations of the past as a sort of theological shorthand. If it is true that many believers before us, especially those with a high view of God's sovereignty in salvation and a commitment to justification being by grace alone through faith alone because of the finished work of Christ alone, spoke of the pre-fall relationship between God and Adam as a covenant of works, why would we not? If it is because it is exegetically unsound and found wanting, then a dismissal of it is reasonable. But if the covenant of works is rejected because it is a completely foreign concept to the ears of a number of evangelical hearers who are less than familiar with how their spiritual forbearers spoke, then perhaps more education in historical theology is in order in order to appreciate and benefit from the working of the Spirit of God in and through the people of God. In short, our ignorance of commonly accepted historic Christian vocabulary really shouldn't be cause for naively rejecting what is in the end the biblical understanding for our help and God's glory.

The covenant of works as a formalized and mature theological perspective has its history in the time of the Protestant Reformation. This is not to say that the concepts, structure, or reality was created or constructed during the time of the Reformation. It is not that any more than the five *solas* were Reformed inventions. It is that the developed and systematized perspective known as the covenant of works is identified around the time of the sixteenth century.

In answering those who object to the covenant of works being a Reformed invention, Vos goes to lengths to demonstrate that it was in fact a Reformed doctrine and then offers a critique that is most helpful. Vos observes, "But whoever has the historical sense to be able to separate the mature development of a thought from its original sprouting and does not insist that a doctrine be mature at birth, will have no difficulty in recognizing the covenant of works as an old Reformed doctrine."[135]

It is one thing for the covenant to be a Reformed doctrine, but another for it to be biblical. Is there any evidence of "sprouting" to be found prior to the reformers? The answer is yes! Michael Horton highlights three key figures from far before the reformation:

> The same emphases may be found in Irenaeus, where he not only affirms an Adamic covenant but distinguishes between an "economy of law" or "law of works" (which he associates with Adam in the prelapsarian situation and then again with Israel in the "Mosaic economy" or "legal dispensation") and a "Gospel covenant." John of Damascus adds, "It was necessary, therefore, that man should first be put to the test (for man untried and unproved would be worth nothing), and being made perfect by the trial through the observance of the command should thus receive incorruption as the prize of his virtue." In the West, Augustine also

[135] Geerhardus Vos, Redemptive History and Biblical Interpretation: The Shorter Writings of Geerhardus Vos, ed. Richard B. Gaffin Jr. (Phillipsburg: P&R, 1980), 237.

> clearly anticipates the covenant of works/covenant of grace scheme, as, for example, in his comment that "the *first covenant* was this, unto Adam: 'Whensoever thou eatest thereof, thou shalt die the death,'" and this is why all of his children "are breakers of God's covenant made with Adam in paradise" (emphasis added).[136]

In addition, "the seeds of the covenantal approach can be easily discerned in Philipp Melanchthon, Heinrich Bullinger, Martin Bucer, and John Calvin."[137]

Beyond the early reformers, the covenant of works has enjoyed wide acceptance by those who are sympathetic to the Protestant reformers. Major theological figures include Zacharias Ursinus (1534-1583), Caspar Olevian (1536-1587), Johannes Cocceius (1609-1669), Herman Witsius (1636-1708), John Owen (1616-1683), Charles Hodge (1797-1878), Herman Bavinck (1854-1921), J. Gresham Machen (1881-1937), and Louis Berkhof (1873-1957).[138] The scope of acceptance has not been limited to Presbyterian and Congregationalist types either. Two of the most famous if not the most famous Baptists were ardent promoters of the covenant of works. Those two are John Bunyan (1628-1688) and Charles Spurgeon (1834-1892). Another notable Baptist is James Petigru Boyce (1827-1888) of The Southern Baptist Theological Seminary. In his *Abstract of Systematic Theology*, published in 1887, he states that "The fall of Man occurred when he was on probation under the Covenant of works."[139]

---

[136] Michael S. Horton, *The Christian Faith: A Systematic Theology for Pilgrims on the Way* (Grand Rapids: Zondervan, 2011), Kindle Electronic Edition: Location 11097-11106; emphasis in original.

[137] Ibid, Kindle Location 11112-11114.

[138] J. Ligon Duncan, *Introduction to Covenant Theology* (Charlotte, NC: Reformed Theological Seminary, 2014), 12, iBook. See also J. Ligon Duncan, "History of Covenant Theology" (sermon, First Presbyterian Church, Jackson, MS, September 3, 1998), accessed December 31, 2015, http://www.fpcjackson.org/resource-library/classes-and-training/history-of-covenant-theology and R. Scott Clark, "A Brief History of Covenant Theology," accessed December 31, 2015, http://spindleworks.com/library/CR/clark.htm.

[139] James P. Boyce, *Abstract of Systematic* (1887).

Earlier dispensationalist writers such as Lewis Sperry Chafer and C. I. Scofield affirmed that Adam was in a covenantal relationship with God before the fall. "Before the fall, Adam was related to God by a covenant of works" is what Chafer says in his systematic theology.[140]

Awareness of past adherents is not the same as biblical proof. But it is hopefully reason for us to humbly consider the conclusions and formulations of previous generations who surely thought of themselves as possessing the guidance of the Spirit as we ourselves claim.

OBJECTIONS

A number of objections have been surfaced and in some cases addressed already. Related as well as additional attention to objections will be considered here.

SALVATION NOT BY WORKS

Sometimes it is objected that eternal life cannot be gained by obedience or works given the Apostle Paul's clear teaching that "by the works of the law no one will be justified" (Gal 2:16). This is in contrast to the way that sinners are justified which is "through faith in Jesus Christ," but it is not in isolation from any works whatsoever given that it is Jesus and his perfect and obedient work that one is to trust in. No sinner's work will be righteous and therefore they could never be justified by their obedience to the law. It is impossible for them to keep the law for justification, which is why Paul says what he does in Galatians 2. Yet is there anyone about whom this does not apply? It would not apply to Jesus the righteous (1 Jn 2:1) nor

---

http://founders.org/library/boyce1/ch22/ (accessed November 2, 2015).

[140] Lewis Sperry Chafer, *Systematic Theology* (Dallas: Dallas Theological Seminary, 1948), 42. Scofield's note on Genesis 2:16 in *The Scofield Reference Bible* refers to Adam's relationship to God as covenantal.

would it have applied to a pre-fall Adam who was part of God's "very good" creation (Gn 1:31).

There is something commendable about a Christian being uncomfortable, if not alarmed, when hearing the words salvation and works in the same sentence unless "*is not by*" separates the "salvation" and "works." The commendable nature of such a response however, is forsaken if it is misapplied and misapplied it is if it requires that salvation has nothing to do with works. After all, it is unequivocally true that salvation comes to sinners as the result of the work of Jesus. Salvation is therefore without hesitation by works for *it is by the works of Christ* that sinners find salvation (e.g. the work of propitiating, the work of reconciling, and the work of redeeming to name a few).

What is not commendable is any attempt to misrepresent advocates of the covenant of works as if they are promoting what would typically be understood by the label "works salvation." A case in point is the book *An Introduction to Classical Evangelical Hermeneutics* edited by dispensationalist Mal Couch.[141] Such labels are not fitting because Adam is in his pre-fall condition and therefore sin has not become a reality and no sin deserving judgment has been committed to be saved from. This is why theologians are careful to describe Adam as being in a state of unconfirmed holiness or something along those lines. Great care is taken to reflect the biblical teaching in such a way that maintains the integrity of the entire corpus. Implying that the covenant of works promotes a form of works salvation is an easy way to win unwitting disciples for oneself. But it simply is not what is being taught, implied, or believed.

DESIRE FOR GRACE BEFORE SIN

Some reject the covenant of works because it does not reflect grace, but law. There are at least a couple of different strains to this

---

[141] Mal Couch, An Introduction to Classical Evangelical Hermeneutics (Grand Rapids: Kregel, 2000), 159.

perspective. It is said that if God is gracious then all that he does is out of grace, including create as well as relate to Adam. The argument states further that since God was not obligated to create Adam, his relationship with him must have been gracious.[142]

The traditional covenant of works perspective heartily concurs that God was not obligated to create, but prefers to reserve the designation of grace for the arena of sin whereby God freely gives to sinners what they do not deserve. Reasons for such a reservation include the following: First, the normative use of grace in Scripture is in reference to God relating to sinners (Eph 2:1-10). Second, the description of the representative heads in Romans 5 are not described in terms of grace in their standing before God, but obedience. Third, the exaltation of Jesus, the last and victorious Adam, is not described in terms of Him gaining such a status because God freely gave him what he did not earn or deserve. In fact, the opposite is the case. It was the work of Jesus that led to his exaltation. Philippians 2 is a case in point: "And being found in human form, he humbled himself by becoming obedient to the point of death, even death on a cross. Therefore God has highly exalted him and bestowed on him the name that is above every name" (Phil 2:8–9).

A more careful word choice describing God's positive disposition toward his created beings before the fall would be what notable Westminster divines utilized. They spoke of "voluntary condescension on God's part." Following Westminster's lead, Michael Horton prudently avoids utilizing words like grace or mercy and instead opts for "condescension, goodness, and kindness."[143] He

---

[142] J. V. Fesko demonstrates that when certain seventeenth century Reformed writers like John Ball (1585-1640) did speak of grace as something shown by God before the fall, it was not in a redemptive sense. Rather, it was a demonstration of divine condescension (J. V. Fesko, *The Theology of the Westminster Standards: Historical Context and Theological Insights* (Wheaton: Crossway, 2014), 138-141. The fact that these men maintained a clear-cut distinction between the perfect obedience demanded by the law and the eternal life freely offered to sinners in the gospel is important. It is important because it shows that those who advocate a blending of faith and works cannot find legitimate support from the Westminster divines.

[143] Michael S. Horton, "Engaging N.T. Wright and John Piper" in *Justified: Modern*

goes on to say "Yet it was not a *gracious* covenant, because grace (like mercy) is God's attitude toward transgressors."[144]

John Murray is often cited as a covenant theologian who took issue with Covenant Theology in part and rejected the covenant of works in its traditional form. Indeed Murray said that Covenant Theology "needs recasting." He did so out of a conviction that all of God's interactions with humanity are gracious.[145] This writer wonders how much if any of Murray's pushback was in response to excessive striving for discontinuity trending in Dispensationalism.[146]

Regardless of the reasoning, Murray's call for recasting and pursuant distaste for traditional labels was not enough to alter the essence of his theological perspective on this point. In fact, his exegetical work in Romans 5 stands to this day as a classic argument for representative headship.[147] However, the recast of Murray is considered to be what cast the door wide open for those who would come after him. Unlike Murray, some of his followers have blended law and grace (or law and gospel) resulting in outright denials of justification by faith alone.

Norman Shepherd, following Murray at Westminster Seminary, barged through the open door that had set aside the covenant of works and its sharp distinction from grace and with it the parallel "law and gospel" paradigm. Lacking Murray's strong commitment to representative headship that functionally held things on track for maintaining a Protestant perspective on justification, Shepherd brought consistency to the blending of works and grace (as well as

---

Reformation Essays on the Doctrine of Justification, ed. Ryan Glomsrud and Michael S. Horton, (Escondido: Modern Reformation, 2010), 12.

[144] Ibid; emphasis in original.

[145] John Murray, *The Covenant of Grace: A Biblico-Theological Study* (Tyndale Press, 1954), n.p. http://www.the-highway.com/Covenant_Murray.html (accessed November 1, 2015).

[146] For a discussion of conflicts between Lewis Sperry Chafer and John Murray provoked by Murray's criticisms, see John D. Hannah, *An Uncommon Union: Dallas Theological Seminary and American Evangelicalism* (Grand Rapids: Zondervan, 2009), 121. See also John Murray, *Principles of Conduct: Aspects of Biblical Ethics* (Grand Rapids, MI: Eerdmans, 1957), 264.

[147] John Murray, *The Imputation of Adam's Sin* (Grand Rapids: Eerdmans, 1959).

law and gospel), albeit an unfortunate consistency. Justification was portrayed as the result of an obedient faith that amounts to faith plus obedience bringing justification.[148] From a similar perspective of a pre-fall grace, Murray and Shepherd drew far different conclusions with Murray remaining traditional in his *sola fide* conviction and Shepherd sounding downright Romanist.

Daniel Fuller is another person associated with collapsing traditional law and grace distinctions that would then demand grace being demonstrated before the fall. Fuller is responding to Dispensationalism and what he considers to be its artificial and frequent divisions between different dispensations.[149] Pushback to radical discontinuity associated with forms of Dispensationalism has been applauded and not without reason. But Fuller overreaches.

Another factor thought to be influencing Fuller's rejection of the traditional distinction between divine law and grace is Karl Barth. Barth is known for being radically against any real distinction as would have been traditionally upheld by Protestants. As Cornelis Venema observes,

> Not only does Barth regard the biblical account of creation and fall to be non-historical *saga*, but he also resists any suggestion of a *transition in history from wrath to grace subsequent to the fall into sin.* From the beginning, God's dealings with the creature are pre-eminently and exclusively *gracious*. There is no change that occurs in history in the relationship between God and the creature because of the fall into sin.[150]

---

[148] For more on the Shepherd controversy see O. Palmer Robertson, *The Current Justification Controversy*, (Unicoi, TN: The Trinity Foundation, 2003). Also see W. Robert Godfrey, "Westminster, Justification, and the Reformed Confessions," in *The Pattern of Sound Doctrine: Systematic Theology at the Westminster Seminaries, Essays in Honor of Robert B. Strimple*, ed. David VanDrunen (Phillipsburg: P&R, 2004), 136-143 and D. G. Hart, *Between the Times: The Orthodox Presbyterian Church in Transition, 1945-1990* (Willow Grove, PA: Committee for the Historian of the Orthodox Presbyterian Church, 2011), 233-255.
[149] See Daniel Fuller, The Unity of the Bible (Grand Rapids: Zondervan, 1992) and Daniel Fuller, Gospel and Law: Contrast or Continuum - The Hermeneutics of Dispensationalism and Covenant Theology (Grand Rapids: Eerdmans, 1980).
[150] Cornelis P. Venema, "Recent Criticisms of the Covenant of Works in the Westminster

Barth's influence may also shed some light on why some theologians blend law with grace and grace with law and thereby find the covenant of works so problematic.

When viewed in light of the likes of Shepherd, Fuller, and Barth, Meredith Kline's criticisms of recasting the traditional law based covenantal relationship existing before the fall into a grace before fall perspective seem fitting. He argues that grace is not only unmerited favor, but is de-merited:

> Theologically it is of the greatest importance to recognize that the idea of demerit is an essential element in the definition of grace. In its proper theological sense as the opposite of law-works, grace is more than unmerited favor. That is, divine grace directs itself not merely to the absence of merit but to the presence of demerit. It addresses and overcomes violation of divine commandment. It is a granting of blessing, as an act of mercy, in spite of previous covenant breaking by which man has forfeited all claims to participation in the kingdom and has incurred God's disfavor and righteous wrath.[151]

Unfortunately, however, gospel grace has been commonly defined by the term unmerited. Then, when unmerited is also used for the divine benevolence in creation an illusion of similarity, if not identity, is produced. As a result the term grace gets applied to God's creational goodness. And the mischief culminates in the argument that since "grace" is built into the human situation at the outset, the covenant that ordered man's existence could not be a covenant of works, for works is the opposite of grace. If we appreciate the forensic distinctiveness of grace we will not thus confuse the specific concept of (soteriological) grace with the beneficence expressed in the

---

Confession of Faith," Mid-America Journal of Theology Vol. 9/3 (Fall 1993): 165-198; emphasis in original.

[151] Meredith Kline, Kingdom Prologue: Genesis Foundations for a Covenantal Worldview, (Eugene: Wipf and Stock Publishers, 2006), 113.

creational endowment of man with his ontological dignity. We will perceive that God's creational manifestation of goodness was an act of divine love, but not of grace. And we have seen that the presence of paternal love in a covenantal arrangement is no impediment to its being a covenant of works.[152]

TERMINOLOGY

One of the more common features of the covenant of works that is targeted for criticism is its title. While there are other titles that can be and are sometimes utilized, "covenant of works" has not been used without reason. Cornelius Venema offers insightful analysis on the matter in calling for the need to counterbalance the designation "covenant of works" with a complementary designation such as "covenant of life" or even "covenant of favor." For after all, the covenant concerned that which was initiated and established by God for communion with him. Also featured however, is the absolute obligation to obey. Such an obligation is to be done out of heartfelt devotion, but obligation it is nonetheless. It is a *work* that must occur according to divine law. Therefore, the "covenant of works" aligns with the spirit of what is required.[153] The both/and as opposed to the either/or is once again helpful in the discussion as it steers readers away from the false choices thrust upon us in objections posed against the covenant of works.

ADAM ALREADY HAD LIFE

Another affront to a covenant of works with Adam for eternal life is the fact that Adam already had life. This surfaces another occasion where understanding the Genesis account calls for drawing upon the work of inspired interpreters and more specifically Paul's typological comparison in Romans 5. The life that Jesus brings to His people is not life that may end or is in any way in jeopardy of being lost.

---

[152] Ibid, 114.
[153] Venema, "Recent Criticisms;" emphasis in original.

Rather, the life that the last Adam secured through His obedience is "eternal life" (5:21). Given the parallels, it can and should be concluded that Adam was to obey and bring life for his people, a kind of life that was different from what he already had.

Genesis is not silent on this and in fact offers support for Adam not yet having eternal life. Adam was alive and was the pinnacle of God's very good creation. But Adam did not have eternal life, the life coming from the tree of life (cf. Gn 3:22; Rv 22:2).

NEVER CALLED A COVENANT

If the covenant of works is not in the Bible, then no one should believe it to be biblical. Such is fair enough rationale. But could it be that something that is in the Bible and therefore biblical is conveniently summarized by thoughtful Bible teachers with a title not used by the Bible itself? All Christians who believe in the Trinity heartily answer in the affirmative! There are labels we use to describe biblical realities even though the title itself is not used in the Scripture.

But what about calling something a covenant when the Bible does not expressly label it a covenant? This is slightly different than the analogy with the Trinity because "trinity" is an altogether extra-biblical name never used in the Bible. Covenant is in fact used to describe covenants such as the Abrahamic, Davidic, Old and New Covenants. Dispensationalists sometimes insist that it is untenable to call something a covenant when the Bible does not use the tag. Here is an example from Mal Couch:

> Dispensationalists respond that *nowhere does the Bible call Adam's obedience a kind of covenant*...According to the biblical evidence gleaned from the limited verses about Adam in Genesis, dispensationalists consider the pre-Fall a period of innocence in which Adam was sinless and was commanded not to eat of a certain tree. God related to Adam in this innocent condition. *But in no way can this be called a covenant relationship in the normal sense of the words.*

> *Dispensationalists have far more evidence for calling the period the dispensation of innocence than do covenant theologians for calling it the covenant of works.*[154]

Saying *nowhere* is necessary sometimes, but it can also embarrass when the data does not match dogmatic assertions. As has already been highlighted, when Israel is being chastised for her betrayal these words come: "But like Adam they transgressed the covenant; there they dealt faithlessly with me" (Hos 6:7). Maybe it should be interpreted differently than "the normal sense of the words" (to quote Couch) and the argument does not stand or fall with this text, but it certainly calls the "nowhere" statement into question. What about the declaration that "in no way can this be called a covenant relationship in the normal sense of the words"? Surely, as has been outlined time and time again, one can find the covenant motif in Genesis. Long-time professor at Dallas Theological Seminary, S. Lewis Johnson highlights the covenantal elements here:

> Now there is certainly a thread here, because we read if Adam eats of the Tree of the Knowledge of Good and Evil in the day that he eats of it he shall surely die. So here is an agreement between two persons with stipulations of performance, there is a promise of a reward, and there is also a promise of the sanction of a penalty. Now that is what a covenant is. So even though the term is not used what we do have in Genesis chapter 2 is a covenant...[155]

When dispensationalists attempt to utilize the "it is not explicitly labeled a covenant in Genesis" argument, are they unaware that it is common for fellow dispensationalists to affirm the so-called

---

[154] Couch, *Evangelical Hermeneutics*, 159-160; emphasis added.

[155] S. Lewis Johnson, *The Edenic Covenant* (Sermon Transcript). http://www.sljinstitute.net/sermons/eschatology/pages/eschatology_8.html (accessed November 27, 2010). Johnson affirms all three covenants of Covenant Theology. His series of lectures comparing Dispensationalism and Covenantalism offer help to those who may listen to someone within dispensational circles. http://sljinstitute.net/category/the-divine-purpose/

"Edenic covenant" and "Adamic covenant" even though the word covenant is absent from the texts utilized?[156]

If one wonders about the legitimacy of utilizing the title "covenant" for something that Genesis itself does not label as such, one need only look as far as the undisputed Davidic Covenant for a counterpart. The Davidic Covenant is established in 2 Samuel 7 even though it is not called a covenant in the text where it first occurs. For that one has to consult the Psalms in Psalm 89: "You have said, 'I have made a covenant with my chosen one; I have sworn to David my servant: 'I will establish your offspring forever, and build your throne for all generations' *Selah*" (Ps 89:3–4).

Likewise, would an objector who says there cannot be a covenantal relationship between God and Adam because Genesis does not label it as such, conclude the same thing about the glory of God? After all, the glory of God is never mentioned as such in the book of Genesis. Yet one would be completely out of touch with reality if he or she concluded that God's glory were not on display throughout Genesis.

In response to John Murray's criticism of the covenant of works given that Genesis does not explicitly label it a covenant, Carl Trueman observes that "From a historical perspective, such criticism misses an important historical point: the covenant of works was not developed simply by exegeting Genesis 1 and 2; it arose more out of reflection on the Pauline epistles than on the creation account…"[157]

---

[156] Tommy Ice says "Even though not called a covenant in the Genesis text the components of a covenant can be observed in the text." http://digitalcommons.liberty.edu/cgi/viewcontent.cgi?article=1002&context=pretrib_arch (accessed October 14, 2015). This perspective is not unique to Ice. Arnold G. Fruchtenbaum is another dispensationalist who sees an Edenic and Adamic covenant in Genesis even though they are not explicitly labeled covenants in Genesis. Where they disagree is the support of Hosea 6:7. Ice utilizes it to support the so called Adamic covenant whereas Fruchtenbaum sees it as supporting the Edenic. http://www.messianicassociation.org/ezine17-af.covenants.htm (accessed October 14, 2015).

[157] Carl Trueman, "Atonement and the Covenant of Redemption" in *From Heaven He Came and Sought Her: Definite Atonement in Historical, Biblical, Theological, and Pastoral Perspective*,

Speaking of John Murray's desire to call the covenant of works an "administration" instead of its traditional name, Jonty Rhodes offers this refreshingly lighthearted rejoinder: "Well, OK. I tend to think this is a bit like calling a cow a domesticated ungulate of the subfamily Bovine. If it's black, white and moos, it's a cow. If you've got God, human beings and conditions with an accompanying threat and an implied blessing, you've got a covenant."[158]

LEGALISM

The accusation that the covenant of works and the greater structure of Covenant Theology within which it resides is legalistic makes some sense for the evangelical. After all, any discussion not to mention grasp of the law or commandments can be remote. To then say anything about a law from God that must be upheld in order for there to be salvation, is likely altogether foreign.

But is it actually the case that Covenant Theology is law centered whereas other brands of theology are grace centered or Christ centered? A sample statement from New Covenant theologian A. Blake White indicates that he thinks so. He says that "Covenant Theology, on the other hand, can be described as being 'law centered."[159] If White meant by this that the covenant of works is a law covenant that must be kept in order for there to be eternal life or that covenant theologians commonly call for believers to obey the moral law of God as an expression of worship and out of gratitude for what Christ has done in fulfilling the law on behalf of those who believe, then the point would be well made that Covenant Theology is "law centered." But the supposed law centeredness of Covenant Theology is made out to be anything but positive in this case, especially when the choice is between what is presented as the

---

ed. David Gibson and Jonathan Gibson (Wheaton: Crossway, 2013), 216.

[158] Jonty Rhodes, Raiding the Lost Ark: Recovering the Gospel of the Covenant King, (Nottingham: Inter-Varsity, 2013), 29-30.

[159] A. Blake White, *What is New Covenant Theology?: An Introduction,* (Frederick, MD: New Covenant Media, 2012), 38.

supposed Christ centeredness of New Covenant Theology and the law centeredness of Covenant Theology. And if Christ centeredness were not enough, the fact that love is the primary emphasis over and against that of law, surely is! For White says that "This means we are not primarily about law, but love!"[160]

But could it be that such arguments are in actuality arguments for the true graciousness of Covenant Theology over and against its accuser? This writer believes so. To state that New Covenant Theology is Christ centered whereas traditional Covenant Theology is law centered is quite a claim. It is quite a claim to make in a book that does not really do anything to substantiate the given declaration. But given his earlier statement, it is difficult to imagine one being more law centered than White himself. The statement calling for closer attention is "This means we are not primarily about law, but love." Did not the Lord Jesus himself affirm that the very essence of the law is love? Indeed he did:

> But when the Pharisees heard that he had silenced the Sadducees, they gathered together. And one of them, a lawyer, asked him a question to test him. "Teacher, which is the great commandment in the Law?" And he said to him, "You shall love the Lord your God with all your heart and with all your soul and with all your mind. This is the great and first commandment. And a second is like it: You shall love your neighbor as yourself. On these two commandments depend all the Law and the Prophets" (Mt 22:34–40).

Pitting law against love is common in pop culture, but is a massive categorical error for anyone teaching the Bible. The very thing that the law calls for is love. For a system boasting in Christ centered superiority, the lack of awareness regarding what Christ himself said about the law is incongruous. What sounds to be a pious criticism

---

[160] Ibid, 36.

against Covenant Theology ends up revealing a sophomoric shallowness of understanding.

In reality, Covenant Theology is anything but lacking in Christ centeredness. The covenant of works is definitely heavy on law as Adam is formally obligated to obey God and thereby love God with heart, soul, mind, and strength. Such is the good and righteous requirement that never can or will change. Yes, this is steeped in law, but it is the very essence of what is right as it maintains the creature/creator distinction and calls for giving to God what is good and right as it is in accordance with the good divine law. What is in fact Christ centered is the reality of Jesus, the last Adam (1 Cor 15:45), perfectly obeying and thereby fulfilling the law (Mt 5:17) by loving God with heart, soul, mind, and strength. The genius of Covenant Theology is tied to the magnificence of Jesus being central to all things in the unfolding of God's drama of redemption. It is Jesus who not only fulfills all righteousness (law), but who likewise atones for all of our trespasses against the divine law.

It is difficult to determine the degree to which White represents the precise views of his fellow New Covenant writers. However, he is apparently in the ballpark given numerous endorsements including ones from Thomas Schreiner, Stephen Wellum, and Jason Meyer.[161]

Ridding any and all fears of legalism should be the partner to the covenant of works which is the covenant of grace. The covenant of grace expresses that salvation is entirely of the Lord (Jon 2:9) and therefore not merited in the least by sinners. But there is no grace to be shown to sinners apart from the fulfillment of the covenant of works by Jesus. The covenant of grace is the subject matter of the next chapter.

---

161 This writer found *Kingdom Through Covenant: A Biblical-Theological Understanding of the Covenants* (Wheaton: Crossway, 2012) by Peter Gentry and Stephen Wellum, a book also promoting New Covenant Theology, to be far more sympathetic to the covenant of works even if not affirming it outright.

NOT A MORAL TEST

N.T. Wright rejects the covenant of works for what appears to be two reasons. First, a denial of a historical Adam in anything resembling a traditional understanding leaves the covenant of works substantively pointless for him. This is the catalyst for Wright's criticism of Albert Mohler. In reference to a quote from Mohler, Wright says, "I think the "covenant of works' line is a kind of 2+2 = 5 thing."[162]

Second, rejecting the covenant of works by Wright is further fueled by a rejection of Adam being under any sort of moral test. He is quoted as saying,

> The point is that if you start, not with Adam and a "moral test," but with Adam and Eve and a vocation (see Psalm 8), then a lot of things in Paul look significantly different. There is more to Paul—and to Genesis—than you might have thought. It all works, it's all good, it's all about God's grace—and it's about a justification through which humans are "put right" in order to get the original project back on track, so that we might be "putting-right" people for the world. That's something that's often been strangely absent from a Westminster Confession type of theology.[163]

It is no wonder his views have been labeled "new perspectives" for indeed they are. Adam was not under a moral test? Instead it was a vocation for Adam and Eve? The "instead" is really a false choice forced upon us by Wright. The truth is, it was through Adam's one act of disobedience (read moral failure) that plunged the human race into a state of guiltiness (Rom 5:18-19). This need not be separated from the vocation of Adam and Eve, but it must be seen as having a disastrous influence upon it afterward.

---

[162] Jonathan Merrit, "N.T. Wright on the Bible and Why He Won't Call Himself an Inerrantist," *Religion News* (June 2014), http://jonathanmerritt.religionnews.com/2014/06/02/n-t-wright-bible-isnt-inerrantist/#sthash.GqHrAKQD.dpuf (accessed July 1, 2015).
[163] Ibid.

Without the historic distinction between the covenant of works and the covenant of grace, neither the divine law nor divine grace remains either law or grace. Instead, there is a blurring that says, "it's all good, it's all about God's grace" and then we are in actuality working for our final justification.

PRACTICAL IMPORTANCE

UNDERSTANDING

The covenant of works provides one with a biblical framework for understanding God, the Bible, and the gospel. God the creator has chosen to relate to his image bearers covenantally with Adam being the federal head. This good arrangement ended badly in defiance against the benevolent creator sovereign. He is therefore just in his condemnation for covenant violation and therefore is not in any way obligated to show mercy. Strictest judgment is called for and fair. This provides a backdrop for understanding the bad things that happen in this cursed world as it relates to what is reasonable and in relationship to God. Given that Adam was the federal representative of the entire human race, we can understand why everyone following Adam has been in a state of conflict with God apart from the gospel. Of course believers in Jesus have a fuller perspective on the provision God graciously makes in Christ and can see that God is both the just and the justifier of the one who has faith in Jesus (Rom 3:26).

Many valuable insights have been drawn from the Bible by those who do not grasp the covenant of works. However, to see the federal perspective articulated in Romans 5 and other texts is to be able to comprehend the Bible in part and whole in a magnificent way, the intended way. To read the Bible from the perspective of the covenant of works being violated by Adam and fulfilled by the long awaited last Adam is to read the Bible the way it was intended to be read. To have this covenantal hermeneutic in place (yes, this writer will happily say this!) is to show interpretive integrity according to divine authorial intent and is to therefore be blessed with legitimate understanding.

The gospel is the good news regarding the work of Jesus for sinners. Grasping the significance of what it means comes from understanding his work as the last Adam, the one who fulfills the covenant of works. Sinners no longer relate to God in Adam, but in Christ. His perfect work is wonderfully understood through the lens offered to us from the covenant of works paradigm. In his standard work on justification, James Buchanan underscores the significance of understanding the covenant of works:

> Hence the careful study of the Law, as a covenant of works, is necessary at all times to the right understanding of the Gospel, as a covenant of grace: and it is peculiarly seasonable in the present age, when the eternal Law of God is supposed, by some, to have been abrogated, and, by others, to have been modified or relaxed. We must believe that the Law of God, in all its spirituality and extent, is still binding, if we are to feel our need of the Gospel of Christ; and we must be brought to tremble under 'the revelation of wrath,' if we are ever to obtain relief and comfort from 'the revelation of righteousness.[164]

DISCERNMENT

In order to avoid the bewitching of gospel attackers, grasping the covenant of works plays a protective role. The result is that one can know why "bad things happen to good people" as the saying goes, that nothing shy of perfect obedience is required for justification, and that only the imputed righteousness of Jesus can fulfill such a requirement. Any and all other answers to the human predicament are dangerous non-answers. This means that understanding the

---

[164] James Buchanan, The Doctrine of Justification: An Outline of its History in the Church and of its Exposition from Scripture (Amazon Digital Services, 2010), Kindle Electronic Edition: Location 471-475.

federal headship of the two Adams will provide the necessary framework for understanding just why it is that salvation is by grace alone, through faith alone, in the finished work of Christ alone.

WORSHIPING

To see that salvation is due to the work of another is to see him as the object of praise. This is what happens when sinners see Jesus as the one who was not only tested, but who fulfilled the law representatively so that his righteousness would be imputed to everyone who believes in him. The difference between this and anything less is massive. For sinners to see that they are justified because of the righteous work of Jesus in fulfilling the law is also a catalyst for worshipping God for his righteousness. Logically, such praise should not be offered if in fact God justifies sinners who offer so-called "evangelical obedience" (see Rom 2:13 discussion above). After all, it would then mean that God declares righteous apart from true righteousness. Besides being unjust, any such action from God would render him less than praiseworthy. But praise be to God, Jesus *is the doer of the law!*

RELATING

The relationships that people have are naturally governed by the principle of law, at least by and large. Individuals relate to others positively or negatively based upon behavior. If someone treats another in a way that fails to meet expectations, the relationship is effected negatively whereas if expectations are met, positively. In other words, if the laws are kept, things are good and if the laws are violated, things are bad. The challenge is with the participants inability to fully uphold relationship laws such as love, loyalty, and honestly. How can the covenant of works help with such relationships? First, it can help by explaining why people relate in less than ideal ways. Second and less obvious, it can enable believers to look further than the offending party's offenses and to see them "in Christ." This can mean that we imitate the perspective of God in seeing sinners as united to Christ for righteousness as opposed to seeing fellow believers as under a kind of covenant of works (God's or ours).

ASSURING

While Martin Luther may have reminded the devil of his baptism when he felt assaulted, this writer suspects that a more frightening weapon for the accuser of the brethren is a reminder of the one who fulfilled the law for his people as the last Adam! What could be more assuring than a finished work, the finished work of the last Adam? The fact that the Lord Jesus Christ's work is complete and that it is complete as the representative of his elect people is the ultimate source of assurance. To know that God is not counting trespasses against those who trust in his Son is the greatest source of assurance (2 Cor 5:19). How different this is from a system offering assurance primarily to those who measure up to God's standards, who obey his law. Assurance does not come from being a doer of the law in the Romans 2 sense given that it must be perfect. Rather, assurance comes from the doer of the law whose work is done for his own![165]

HELPING

Christians want to help people. From pastors to parishioners, as those who have been helped in the greatest sense, Christians want to help others to know God, his ways, and what it means to experience his salvation in the most extensive sense. One of the greatest ways we can help others to understand Christ and Christianity is to help them to see why things are the way that they are "in Adam" and to see the extraordinary hope that is found "in Christ." This is nothing shy of what is wrapped up in the covenant of works. Such help spans

[165] This is not to deny the place of a more subjective assurance arising from the actual transformation of life seen in the lives of believers as the Holy Spirit produces fruit in his or her life (cf. 1 John). Such is not the point of Romans 2 nor is it the primary source of assurance, which should only be reserved for the objective and completed work of Christ.

from understanding the Bible, God, self, Jesus, salvation, neighbor, and beyond.

We have seen that Covenant Theology's federal headship is biblical, historical, and helpful. As far as being biblical, the covenantal relationship between Adam and God is not founded upon obscure texts. Instead, the biblical proofs are clear and clearly teach that Adam, the covenant head of the human race, acted in unrighteousness and thereby brought condemnation. Jesus on the other hand, represented all who would ever believe as he fulfilled the divine law and thereby secured justification. These realities have a long history of being seen as vital to justification *sola fide* and therefore vital to the gospel itself. The church can benefit substantially from comprehending and embracing the covenant of works as it seeks to honor the very one who fulfilled all righteousness!

- 4 -

THE COVENANT OF GRACE

The covenant of grace is significant because it demonstrates that a positive relationship between sinners and God is not only possible, but comes to the sinner by God's grace alone on account of the substitutionary work of Christ. Accordingly, this is so regardless of whether the sinner lives before or after the earthly ministry of Jesus. The covenant of grace has enjoyed broad acceptance by many as the best way of explaining the saving work of God. Such a perspective provides tremendous assistance to the reader of Scripture as he or she encounters its various covenants and commands.

In this chapter we will begin by discussing the critical importance of the covenant of grace as it relates to the covenant of works. We will then define the covenant as that which exists between God and elect sinners whereby salvation comes by faith alone in the finished work of Jesus. A brief preview of common objections will be followed by biblical and theological support for the covenant of grace. Such support will focus on the explicit teaching of Scripture that salvation is and always has been by grace alone in the one and only qualified mediator between the covenant Lord and his people. Consideration will be given to various objections relating to biblicism, hermeneutics, continuity/discontinuity, law/gospel, and baptism. Practical aspects of the doctrine will close the chapter.

IMPORTANCE

When describing the crucial significance of the covenant of grace and in particular the need to see it as utterly distinct from the covenant of works, Baptist preacher C. H. Spurgeon offers an outstanding observation:

> The Doctrine of the Divine Covenant lies at the root of all true theology. It has been said that he who well understands the distinction between the Covenant of Works and the Covenant of Grace is a master of divinity. I am persuaded that most of the mistakes which men make concerning the Doctrines of Scripture are based upon fundamental errors with regard to the Covenants of Law and of Grace.[166]

Given the overwhelming number of commands in both the Old and New Testaments, even the commands that specifically tell us that observing them is required for justification (e.g. Rom 2:13 which is engaged elsewhere) and the equally clear declarations of justification being of the ungodly strictly on account of God's grace due to the work of Jesus, it would seem that Mr. Spurgeon knew what he was talking about.

DEFINITION

The definition offered by Louis Berkhof is succinct in saying that "The covenant of grace may be defined as that gracious agreement between the offended God and the offending but elect sinner, in

---

[166] Charles Spurgeon, *The Wondrous Covenant*, (Metropolitan Tabernacle Pulpit, 1912). http://www.spurgeongems.org/vols58-60/chs3326.pdf (accessed October 14, 2015).

which God promises salvation through faith in Christ, and the sinner accepts this believingly, promising a life of faith and obedience."[167]

Berkhof proceeds to highlight five characteristics of the covenant of grace which include the following: 1) It is a gracious covenant, 2) It is a Trinitarian covenant, 3) It is an eternal and therefore unbreakable covenant, 4) It is a particular and not universal covenant, 5) It is essentially the same in all dispensations though its form of administration changes.[168]

Commenting on the distinction between the covenant of grace and the covenant of redemption, John Flavel (1627-1691) highlights two important differences. First, the covenant of grace is "made in Christ betwixt God and us" whereas the covenant of redemption is between Father, Son, and Spirit. Second, "they differ, also in the receptive part, in this it is required of Christ that he should shed his blood, in that it is required of us that we believe."[169]

Given the current controversy over whether or not God showed grace to Adam before the fall (to be discussed elsewhere), it should be noted here that the covenant of grace is traditionally not viewed as concerning pre-fall, but "the offended God and the offending but elect sinner" (see Berkhof above). Specifics regarding the aforementioned controversy are covered when discussing the covenant of works rather than here.

PRELIMINARY OBJECTIONS

Before moving into the arguments for the covenant of grace, preliminary consideration of some objections may prove beneficial.

The obvious objection is that the title "covenant of grace" is not found in Scripture. Predictably then the accusation of it being a hermeneutic forcefully imposed upon Scripture follows. Too much

---

[167] L. Berkhof, *Systematic Theology* (Grand Rapids: Eerdmans, 1938), 277; italics in original.
[168] Ibid, 238.
[169] John Flavel, *The Works of John Flavel*, (Amazon Digital Services, 2011), Kindle Electronic Edition: Location 3617-3622.

continuity due a single and overarching covenant of grace for salvation is another point of protest and it has several points of conflict. First, it may be seen as a threat to the uniqueness of Israel and the uniqueness of the church. Second, this continuity may also be seen as incompatible with the Mosaic law's exclusivity within the Old Testament. Third, the continuity may be seen as demanding infant baptism. Fourth, the continuity afforded by a single covenant of grace would exclude any possibility of salvation ever being according to anything other than grace, even under the old covenant. Such potential objections will be addressed throughout this chapter.

SUPPORT

SOLA GRATIA

The greatest support for the covenant of grace is the unified testimony of Scripture for the salvation of sinners always and only being by God's grace. It is not that salvation comes to some according to their obedience and others by grace. This is fundamental to Paul's argument in Romans 4 for justification not according to the efforts (religious or otherwise) of sinners, but by faith alone in the provision of God, a provision freely given. If anyone was going to be considered righteous according to his own efforts, proud Jewish objectors would hold up the great patriarch "Father Abraham." To which Paul says,

> What then shall we say was gained by Abraham, our forefather according to the flesh? For if Abraham was justified by works, he has something to boast about, but not before God. For what does the Scripture say? "Abraham believed God, and it was counted to him as righteousness." Now to the one who works, his wages are not counted as a gift but as his due. And to the one who does not work but believes in him who justifies the ungodly, his faith is counted as righteousness (Rom 4:1–5).

And if Abraham only serves to prove the point that salvation is exclusively of the Lord and therefore all of grace, the next best exception put forth by the Jewish mind might be David. David, likewise a notorious sinner however, is upheld not as the exception, but further proving the rule: "just as David also speaks of the blessing of the one to whom God counts righteousness apart from works: 'Blessed are those whose lawless deeds are forgiven, and whose sins are covered; blessed is the man against whom the Lord will not count his sin' " (Rom 4:6–8). Salvation is always *sola fide* and therefore entirely gracious.

The covenant of grace is a historic Christian way of explaining the biblical teaching that the sole means for sinners to enjoy a positive relationship with God (recalling from previous discussions that covenant is a relationship concept) is according to his grace.

COVENANTAL UNITY

Two familiar biblical statements whereby God expresses a unique commitment are these: "I will…be God to you" and "I will be their God." These covenantal statements are familiar because they occur repeatedly in both the older and newer Testaments ranging from Genesis to Revelation. In Genesis 17 God declares to Abram

> And I will establish my covenant between me and you and your offspring after you throughout their generations for an everlasting covenant, to be God to you and to your offspring after you. And I will give to you and to your offspring after you the land of your sojournings, all the land of Canaan, for an everlasting possession, and I will be their God" (Gn 17:7–8).

Note these specific features: the expression of devotion is covenantal, is made by God to those who belong to Him according to His grace, and is promised to the people of God both before and after the earthly ministry of Jesus.

In addressing the church at Corinth, Paul applies the covenantal promise: "What agreement has the temple of God with idols? For we are the temple of the living God; as God said, 'I will make my dwelling among them and walk among them, and I will be their God, and they shall be my people' " (2 Cor 6:16).

In the eschaton the promise comes in its fullness as recorded by John the Apostle: "And I heard a loud voice from the throne saying, 'Behold, the dwelling place of God is with man. He will dwell with them, and they will be his people, and God himself will be with them as their God' " (Rv 21:3).

From these occurrences we are led to conclude that the positive relating of God to sinners is covenantal. To therefore describe a positive relationship between God and sinners under the designation "Covenant of grace" corresponds with the biblical data.

SALVATION IS THROUGH ONE ULTIMATE MEDIATOR

Jesus is the one mediator as explicitly stated in in 1 Timothy 2:5: "For there is one God, and there is one mediator between God and men, the man Christ Jesus." The statement is both inclusive and exclusive and as such makes a profound point. The one and only mediator between the one and only God and humanity is Jesus. Any thought of there being another way other than what we know to be the gracious provision of God should not receive so much as a second thought. For even the Old Testament believer was reconciled to God by virtue of Jesus the mediator, albeit in anticipation. They are those described as having committed "transgressions…under the first covenant" (Heb 9:15).

The promise of Genesis 3:15 is where we first hear the good news of a victorious savior. And while an isolated reading may bring more questions than answers, set in a greater context, the answers come: "I will put enmity between you and the woman, and between your offspring and her offspring; he shall bruise your head, and you shall bruise his heel" (Gn 3:15). The messianic expectation can then commence as humanity looks for the coming of the mediator, the one in whom they will trust, the one who will bring them saving grace. In the words of Kline, "The Genesis 3 narrative of the judgment that terminated the original covenantal order in Eden is, therefore, at the same time the record of the inauguration of the new redemptive order of the Covenant of Grace."170

Also terminated is the unholy alliance between Satan and Eve, the relationship entered into by Eve when she agreed with the lies about God. Through the work of Jesus as "the last Adam" (1 Cor 15:45), this gracious promise is realized and as those united to Christ by faith, believers are assured final and sure victory over Satan. As is promised in Romans 16:20 "The God of peace will soon crush Satan under your feet. The grace of our Lord Jesus Christ be with you!"

DIFFERING ADMINISTRATIONS

Covenant is a major if not dominant theme in the Bible. But there are numerous covenants between God and humans and some of these occupy a large role with significant attention being given to them. The Abrahamic, Mosaic, Davidic, and New Covenant occupy a place of major importance in God's redemptive dealings with men and women. Each covenant is uniquely given by God to his people for their good. For them to therefore fall under the banner of the covenant of grace is something similar to what Paul designates as "the covenants of promise" in Ephesians 2:12.

The title "covenant of grace" has provided the church with theological shorthand that can both help disciples keep things graspable as well as guarding against straying from the consistent declaration of Scripture that salvation is of the Lord (Ps 3:8).

---

[170] Meredith Kline, *Kingdom Prologue: Genesis Foundations for a Covenantal Worldview*, (Eugene: Wipf and Stock Publishers, 2006), 143.

OBJECTIONS AND RESPONSES

BIBLICIST

The fact that the title "covenant of grace" is never used in Scripture and therefore should be rejected is a biblicist argument.[171] While it is true that the title is not used, its absence does not make it untrue. As shown elsewhere, extra-biblical titles have been of great assistance to believers in summarizing and categorizing what the Bible teaches on a given subject. "Trinity" is the classic case in point. When casting doubt on the veracity of Covenant Theology, one opponent writes that "the covenant theologian *never* finds in the Bible the terms...covenant of grace."[172] Thankfully the critic does acknowledge some truthfulness to the "ideas and concepts" to the point of saying they "are not unscriptural." It does appear an oddity however that he then goes on to argue against the covenant of grace.

The fact that believers have found it helpful to summarize the covenantal relationship that they and all other believers of every age have enjoyed with God (as demonstrated above) as the "covenant of grace" makes one question the wisdom of jettisoning it.

HERMENEUTICS

Charles Ryrie expresses further concern that "as a result of the covenant of grace idea, Covenant Theology has been forced to place as its most basic principle of interpretation the principle of interpreting the Old Testament by the New."[173] Setting aside the value or lack thereof of utilizing the New Testament in interpreting the Old, the presence of the covenant of grace idea (as Ryrie calls it) does not itself necessitate the practice of interpreting the Old Testament by the New. After all, the Old Testament itself has been

---

[171] See appendix on biblicism for elaboration.
[172] Charles C. Ryrie, *Dispensationalism: Revised and Expanded* (Chicago: Moody, 1995), 189; emphasis in original.
[173] Ibid, 191.

shown to teach salvation by grace alone through Jesus the one mediator (see above).

Likewise, the covenantal relationship between the Lord and believers has been shown to be trans-testamental evidenced with the "I will be their God" formula. Therefore to object on hermeneutical grounds to the covenant of grace as a legitimate label for God's relationship with the elect at all points in history is puzzling. There is one way of salvation which is by grace alone and the relationship between God and his people is described covenantally regardless of whether they are in the Old or the New Testament.

UNIQUENESS OF ISRAEL AND THE CHURCH

Does the covenant of grace force a continuity so as to erase uniqueness between Israel and the church? There is no doubt that a covenant of grace in Covenant Theology sees and highlights the continuity of Scripture and of the way in which God and his people relate. But such continuity does not in itself erase all distinctions. The important distinction that the covenant of grace does eradicate is the manifestly unbiblical distinction between the way in which God justifies.

Acknowledging the continuity that the covenant of grace brings does not come at the expense of all discontinuity. The choice is not a strict either/or. Those of a more theonomic persuasion will in all likelihood opt for far less distinction, but even there, some will exist.[174] More commonly however within Covenant Theology will be an affirmation of the difference and similarity.

Forcing discontinuity for fear of allowing for much of any similarity between Israel and the church has shown itself to be a problem for dispensationalists in the past. Such forced discontinuity is what led Lewis Sperry Chafer, a principal architect in

---

[174] Theonomic is in reference to theonomy, the theological persuasion seeking to "reconstruct society along the lines set forth in the Mosaic Law" (George Thomas Kurian, *Nelson's New Christian Dictionary: The Authoritative Resource on the Christian World* (Nashville, TN: Thomas Nelson Publishers, 2001), electronic ed. Logos Library System.

dispensational thought, to teach that Jesus died for the Jews, but was not raised from the dead for them! While this may protect or strengthen Dispensationalism's desire for radical discontinuity, it cannot be true. It cannot be true because in order to be justified, one must have the resurrection of Jesus. For Romans 4:25 says that Jesus was "raised for our justification." Earlier in the same chapter both Abraham and David are used as examples of those who have been justified so it must be true for them even though they are Old Testament saints. The point of bringing up such an odd teaching from Chafer is to illustrate the incredibly bizarre and massively problematic soteriological conclusions that have stemmed from insistence upon radical discontinuity, the kind which sometimes leads dispensationalists to reject the covenant of grace.[175] It is no wonder that Chafer described the covenant of grace as "far from a Scriptural conception."[176]

MOSAIC LAW NOT GRACIOUS

The covenant of grace is feared by some to interfere with the distinction spoken of by the Apostle Paul between law and grace. According to one critic of Covenant Theology,

> Covenant Theology denies or weakens some of the distinctions which are in the Bible by insisting that distinctions are simply different phases of the same Covenant of Grace. For example, Covenant Theology nullifies the genuine distinction between the Abrahamic Covenant and the Mosaic Covenant (the Law)...But if these two covenants were essentially the same, why did Paul

---

[175] The actual wording Chafer uses is here: "nor are the Old Testament saints ever said to be related thus to the resurrected Christ" (*Systematic Theology*, vol. 4, (Dallas: Dallas Theological Seminary, 1948), 32. One can hope that Chafer actually means something different from what it sounds like he means. This writer confesses that he may be misunderstanding Chafer's intention as it occurs in the context of "proving" the difference between the heavenly people of God and the earthly people of God. Regardless, Chafer is an illustration of the ecclesiological tail wagging the soteriological dog, which has proven to be a poor example to his followers.

[176] Chafer, *Systematic Theology*, Vol. 1, 42.

> emphasize their distinctiveness in Galatians 3? For example, in Galatians 3:18 Paul asserted that if the inheritance is based on the Law of the Mosaic Covenant, it cannot at the same time be based upon the promise of the Abrahamic Covenant.[177]

Covenant Theology teaches that the Mosaic covenant is graciously given by God with all of its types and shadows anticipating fulfillment in Christ, but this is not the same as saying that the Mosaic Law and the Abrahamic promise are the same. Note the difference even in the last sentence as it aligns with the theological point being made by the Apostle Paul. To equate law (in this case Mosaic) with promise would be a massive error. But neither Paul nor Covenant Theology does this when it is said that the Mosaic covenant is an administration of the covenant of grace. God graciously gave the Mosaic Law, but not as a means by which any sinner could ever obey *for eternal life*. Rather, they could be shown their sin and need for a substitute. Saying it was graciously given is not the same as saying that it graciously saves.

Showers criticizes Berkhof for referring to the two covenants as sharing the same essence as covenants. In Berkhof's defense it should be observed that he says more by observing, "But it should be noted that the apostle does not contrast with the covenant of Abraham the Sinaitic covenant as a whole, but only the law as it functioned in this covenant, and this function only as it was misunderstood by the Jews."[178]

The law in particular is in view in Galatians 3 and where law (Mosaic or otherwise!) is viewed as a means by which sinners can justify themselves (in part or whole), it is anything but the same as promissory and therefore not gracious and therefore not the same as the Abrahamic covenant.[179]

---

[177] Renald E. Showers, *There Really is a Difference: A Comparison of Covenant and Dispensational Theology*, (Bellmawr, NJ: Friends of Israel Gospel Ministry, 1990), 20.

[178] L. Berkhof, *Systematic Theology* (Grand Rapids: Eerdmans, 1938), 297.

[179] This project is not addressing the issue of whether or not the Mosaic Law is in one

BAPTISM

Credo Baptists sometimes fear the covenant of grace because of its stress on the unity between the old and new covenant worlds. The rationale is that if there is essential sameness throughout redemptive history then the administration of covenant signs will be greatly the same, specifically baptism will not be reserved for those who personally trust in Christ.

But if the covenant of grace can be defined as Berkhof does above, there is no reason for Baptist reservation. After all, he says that "God promises salvation through faith in Christ, and the sinner accepts this believingly." What follower of Spurgeon would not agree with such a description?

The fact is that there is continuity between the testaments because there is one mediator and the one and only way for sinners to be justified is by faith alone as has been argued by Paul in Romans 4. This does not mean that there are not differences and it certainly does not prove pedobaptism. The intention of this project is not to argue for a particular position on who should be baptized so that will not be undertaken here. It should be noted that the existence of the covenant of grace definitely demands soteriological continuity. But this is far different from unity in all things. The difference in the sign itself makes this point.

EXCLUDES LAW

While some who oppose the covenant of grace do so in part because it includes the Mosaic Law (e.g. Dispensationalists like Showers), others like Daniel Fuller, Norman Shepherd, and

---

sense a republication of the covenant of works, though certain statements that have been made reflect a positive answer to the inquiry. The topic is as important as the debate is raging. Two works addressing opposing sides are *The Law Is Not of Faith: Essays on Works and Grace in the Mosaic Covenant*, ed. Bryan D. Estelle, J. V. Fesko, and David VanDrunen, (Phillipsburg: P&R, 2009) which argues for a form of republication and *Merit and Moses: A Critique of the Klinean Doctrine of Republication* by Andrew Elam, Robert Van Kooten, and Randall Bergquist (Eugene: Wipf & Stock, 2014) argues against republication.

N.T. Wright may object because they fear it to be lacking law.[180] Such fears are substantiated given that the covenant of grace has no place for sinners obeying law in part or whole in order to be justified.

Therefore those who advocate justification by faithfulness such as Fuller, Shepherd, and Wright resist the covenant of grace altogether or at least in its standard formulation. When this covenant is rejected the covenant of works goes along with it. For if the latter requires strict obedience to be fulfilled by Jesus, then salvation comes to the sinner via the covenant of grace freely! The two stand or fall together. To require works for salvation by the sinner is to reject both the covenant of works and the covenant of grace. This happens time and time again in cases where the Reformed doctrine of justification by faith alone in the finished work of Christ alone is compromised. It necessitates a recasting of the covenantal structure into something entirely different.

Therefore when someone like Daniel Fuller rejects the covenant of works, he also rejects the covenant of grace even if he still utilizes the standard verbiage.[181] By collapsing the two into one, grace is no longer grace and law is no longer law. Similar moves are made by Karl Barth as well as others who seek to require that faithfulness instead of faith alone is the means by which sinners are justified.

While the differences among deniers of *sola fide* are vast and beyond our intention here, one unifying factor for everyone from N.T. Wright to Norman Shepherd is the denunciation of the two-covenant perspective of grace and works.

---

[180] This is not to suggest that Fuller, Shepherd, or Wright would verbalize a denial of the covenant of grace. But they do reject the covenant of grace as it is articulated in traditional covenant theology, most specifically in relation to the covenant of works. This is to say that while one may speak of a covenant of grace, if it is not in relation to the covenant of works, it is not actually a covenant of grace in the traditional sense. See "The Covenant of Works" chapter for specifics on the views of the abovementioned authors.

[181] See Daniel Fuller, *The Unity of the Bible: Unfolding God's Plan for Humanity* (Grand Rapids: Zondervan, 2007) and Daniel Fuller, *Gospel & Law: Contrast or Continuum?* (Pasadena: Fuller Seminary Press, 1990). For a critique of Fuller and issues surrounding his novel positions, see Covenant Theology Under Attack by Meredith Kline accessed at the following resource: http://www.opc.org/new_horizons/Kline_cov_theo.html (accessed October 14, 2015).

Besides safeguarding the gospel of grace, the covenant of grace is wonderfully not anti-law. For the covenant of grace brings salvation to sinners because of the perfect obedience of Jesus to the covenant of works. Therefore the righteousness of God in the law is not in the least compromised nor is the purity of God's grace to sinners in the gospel.

PRACTICAL IMPORTANCE

Like the other covenants, the covenant of grace affords the reader of Scripture with a tremendously valuable guide so that he or she is able to read and understand the Bible according to authorial intent in the truest sense. The God who has always and will always save by his grace alone on account of the finished work of Christ alone has made this known thereby blessing the reader and encouraging him or her to keep this in mind on the journey through variegated landscapes which the Bible affords.

GRASPING THE BIBLE

Such grandeur can and has led far too many believers into a state of bafflement when such has not been necessary. If every new Bible reader could receive the pastoral care of being introduced to the God of the Bible as one who relates to the believer by grace and only by grace because of the work of Christ, the recipient would be well served for a lifetime. Unfortunately, many Christians are left to struggle on their own to comprehend until someone either helps them to see what was true all along or until they are able to see the parts and the whole of the Bible clearly enough to relate both forest and trees as they were meant to be seen.

FINDING HOPE

Despair is one thing that will plague all who honestly and realistically see themselves for who they truly are in contrast with the divine law. This is true not just for the unbeliever, but believer also. The potentially devastating consequences are as real as they are frightening. Classic Covenant Theology serves the church and its members well as the best cure for such despair. For not only does Jesus fulfill the law in the covenant of works, the benefits of his atoning sacrifice and righteousness are given freely to believers in the covenant of grace. Samuel Bolton helps us to see the sustaining grace in the covenant of grace with these words:

> Even though the believer falls into sin, yet the law cannot pronounce the curse on him because, as he is not under the law, he is freed from the curse of the law. A man is never afraid of that obligation which is rendered void, the seals torn off, the writing defaced, nay, not only crossed out and cancelled but torn in pieces. It is thus that God has dealt with the law in the case of believers, as touching its power to curse them, to sentence them and condemn.[182]

CURBING PRIDE

Complimenting the joyous cure for despairing offered by the covenant of grace is another likewise needed cure. That cure being a remedy for pride. When sinners see themselves "in Adam" naturally and read the Scripture accordingly with even the greatest of characters likewise destitute when left to themselves, the church will be blessed with relief from pride. To then see that salvation is truly "of the Lord" in all aspects as the covenant of grace makes clear, will likewise foster humility instead of pride.

Having seen that the unified testimony of Scripture is that the covenant Lord saves his elect people *sola gratia* by the exclusive mediatorial work of Jesus, the covenant of grace stands ready to encourage believers and answer objectors.

---

[182] Samuel Bolton, *The True Bounds of Christian Freedom* (1645; repr. Carlisle: Banner of Truth, 1978), 31.

- 5 -

COVENANT THEOLOGY FOR THE CHURCH

There is a great need in the church for Covenant Theology. For it is either largely absent or worse, it is misunderstood and even feared. Many evangelical congregations and pastors simply do not know what they are missing and so they continue down the road of merely pursuing "the next big thing" or weighing down themselves and others with more and more so-called "timeless truths" and principles.

All of this occurs at the expense of reading, preaching, and hearing the Bible according to its actual intended meaning whereby the triune God is unfolding his eternal purpose of reconciling all things through the true and better Adam, the Lord Jesus Christ. This and this alone is *the* timeless truth that brings all other good and important principles into their proper context.

In an effort to assist in the recovery of Covenant Theology for the church, two items will be offered here. One will be a highlighting of what makes Covenant Theology so valuable in the life of the church. This section of the chapter will offer a series of reasons underscoring its worth. The second section will furnish guidelines for implementing Covenant Theology into the life of the church.

One important qualification is that what is said here is dependent upon what has already been discussed. Therefore some reasonable assumptions will be made in what follows.

THE VALUE OF COVENANT THEOLOGY FOR THE CHURCH

The significance of Covenant Theology is challenging to express. There are so many ways in which it can benefit the church that attempts to list them will inevitably mean leaving things out. Nevertheless, with limitations acknowledged, what follows are some of the significant reasons why Covenant Theology is so vital.

IT IS GOD'S WAY OF RELATING TO US

While it may not be quite right to say that Covenant Theology is God's way of relating to us (as the outline point indicates), the point needs to be stressed that God does in fact relate to us *covenantally*. From the human point of view, what could be more important? To ask the question is really to answer it. In order to understand our relationship to God and his to us one must understand the concept of covenant and more specifically the covenantal perspective outlined in classic Covenant Theology. This covers relating to God "in Adam" as well as "in Christ," the last Adam. When one considers how many people are unfamiliar with the biblical concept of the covenant, or Covenant Theology, the need for teaching these subjects becomes clear. If the Bible regularly refers to the concept, we should seek a better understanding of this truth. After all, we are not talking about peripheral issues when considering the very way in which God relates. Similarly, how many evangelicals have given consideration to the fact that the formal relationship between God and Adam is covenantal? Very few is the likely answer. This is problematic given the great importance of the creator/creature distinction, Adam as the head of the human race, as well for a biblical anthropology.

Our relationship to God as the triune God also comes uniquely into view in Covenant Theology, which brings us to the next reason.

IT IS TRINITARIAN

The covenant of redemption in particular has the ability to bring into focus the working of the triune God in an outstanding way that would otherwise be overlooked. It showcases the intra-trinitarian love of God as it highlights the relationship that God himself enjoys. With all of its complexity, the glimpse into such a relationship aids the church in increasing in the knowledge of God and in the worship that corresponds. The following examples demonstrate the need and usefulness of Federal Theology as it relates to the Trinity.

Covenant theology can help Christians recognize that the Holy Spirit is a person, not a thing, and he participates in the planning, execution, and application of our covenantal redemption.

Covenant theology brings God's unity into clear focus as it concerns the work of redemption. Believers are therefore freed from thinking that the desires and aims of the Father, Son, and Spirit are anything less than unified and complementary. Such is commonly not the case outside of Covenant Theology.[183]

How could a professing evangelical conclude that substitutionary atonement amounts to child abuse as happened not long ago?[184] A precise answer is difficult to give. However, we can know that adherence to the covenant of redemption as articulated in the Bible would have guarded against such an error as it explains the Son's agreement concerning his redemptive work even as he gave himself up for sinners.

---

[183] See Amyraldianism and Amyraldian-like perspectives on predestination and universal atonement.

[184] See Steve Chalke and Alan Mann, *The Lost Message of Jesus* (Grand Rapids: Zondervan, 2003), 182-183.

IT IS BIBLICAL

Support does not arise from a simple proof text. But then again few great doctrines of the Christian faith do. Instead, they stand upon the canon of Scripture as its various parts are seen together. Contrary to the accusation of some, Covenant Theology is not the byproduct of allegorizing or spiritualizing the text of the Bible. This has been shown to be anything but the case in passage after passage as they have been examined in context and taken at face value. From Romans 5 to Ephesians 1 to Hosea 6 and the rest, the grand biblical storyline upholds Federal Theology as biblical. There is a real need for believers to see the consistent exegetical and theological basis for Covenant Theology. The primary outcome is edification. A secondary outcome can be the ability to recognize and discern anti-Federal Theology rhetoric for what it is. To reject Federal Theology, that is, Adam and Christ's representative roles in redemptive history as Paul explains in Romans 5, is not merely to disagree with Covenant Theology but ultimately the clear teaching of Scripture.

IT IS HISTORIC

Covenant Theology has a long history where it has been formulated, affirmed, attacked, tested, and refined. A lengthy history is not what makes it true. But such does mean that it has seen enough to have gained a wealth of wisdom. In other words, like a seasoned veteran, there are few new scenarios that have not already been considered. This is part of what comes with maturity whether speaking of people or theological perspectives. Reliability and credible answers no matter the supposed crisis is what can be found. Covenant Theology has shown itself to be the theological perspective that has proven to be *tried* and *true*. As such, it can serve the church for ages to come.

IT MAKES THE BIBLE UNDERSTANDABLE

The Bible is far from simple and in certain ways has proven to be very difficult to understand. Different Testaments, authors, languages, settings, tribes, vocabularies, and covenants are samplings of what makes the Bible a challenge for scholar and Sunday School teacher alike. To say that the Bible is supremely about the glory of God is to make a great observation and one that no serious Bible reader would argue about, but more needs to be said. Covenant Theology offers a perspective for understanding the Bible that keeps both specifics and generalities of the drama in view, all the while remaining faithful to "*the* eternal purpose" of God as it guides the narrative from beginning to end (Eph 3:11).

By making the Bible easier to understand, Covenant Theology serves one of the aims for which it was intended by the Protestant Reformers who sought the codification and development of it. Over and against Rome's confusing blend of law and gospel, a clear articulation of the biblical distinction between the covenant of works and the covenant of grace provides believers with needed clarity. Just such clarity is needed today.

IT UNIQUELY GLORIFIES JESUS

In view of God's eternal purpose being the summing up of all things in Christ, Covenant Theology uniquely calls for all of Scripture to be read with this in view as everything that happens in all of history either anticipates or appreciates the work of Jesus. Correspondingly, the important role of types are kept in check so as not to eclipse the fulfillment they find in Christ *the* antitype. The great King David for example, is kept from being mistakenly elevated to the primacy of place reserved for Christ alone. As unnecessary as this may sound, other approaches to understanding Scripture can fall into just such a trap.

In addition to keeping the lead actor in the drama in his rightful spotlight, the covenants of redemption, works, and grace keep the glory from sinners to reward it to the one and only worthy one. For Christ and Christ alone truly acts righteous and his righteousness comes to sinners by grace and only by grace. The exclusive works counted worthy are his.

IT IS THE SAFEGUARD TO JUSTIFICATION *SOLA FIDE*

Recent controversies relating to justification have led those desiring to uphold the Protestant perspective to historic Federal Theology for help. This is due at least in part because Covenant Theology maintains as essential those elements that justification by faith alone is built upon—the righteousness of Christ as our representative law keeper which is in fulfillment of the covenant of works. The importance of Covenant Theology corresponds to the importance of justification *sola fide* and the gospel that depends upon it. Justification by faith alone is organically connected to realities fundamentally tied to classic Covenant Theology. Therefore, to aid the church in her effort to promote and protect the gospel, Federal Theology must not be marginalized, discounted, or ignored. History reminds us that attacks, confusion, and debate relating to justification will continue, which makes the covenants of redemption, works, and grace perpetually relevant.

Recognizing the place where justification has been protected, defended, and preserved will hopefully lead many to the safe place that is the federal headship of Christ found alone in Covenant Theology.

IT WONDERFULLY ASSURES BELIEVERS

Where does our security rest? If it is within ourselves even in the slightest, assurance simply cannot be sure. Yet a steadfast hope can be found. It can be found "not having a righteousness of my own…but that which comes through faith in Christ, the righteousness from God" (Phil 3:9). When knowledge of such good news is present, doubts and fears can flee and the giver of such a delightful gift can be exalted. Covenant Theology ministers to believers as they struggle with issues related to spiritual security. After all, knowledge of the triune God and the divine oath to save brings reality into perspective, that reality being that salvation is sure. The Spirit *will* seal *all* of those who have been given to the Son by the Father and *not a single one* will be lost (Jn 6:39; Eph 1:13-14). Knowledge of such wonderful certainties fosters unrivaled encouragement to sinners who have been united to Christ. Therefore Covenant Theology is needed as it provides just such knowledge.

IT KEEPS THE MESSAGE ON POINT

One sure way to keep the divine author's message the church's message is to see things through the lenses afforded to us in what has become known as Covenant Theology. Pushback to what has become known as preaching Christ in all of Scripture may be appropriate, but only if Covenant Theology is not true. But if it is, then the Apostle Paul's "to know nothing among you except Jesus Christ" fits like hand to glove! The claims of Jesus regarding the Old Testament speaking of him then also find their reasonable place (Lk 24:44; Jn 5:46).

The church's ministry of preaching, evangelizing, and counseling, can maintain fidelity unto Christ as she remains mindful of this perspective afforded to her. On the contrary, the church can avoid the hopelessness of all other messages that so often only end in the preaching of self (2 Cor 4:5).

GUIDE FOR IMPLEMENTING COVENANT THEOLOGY

The chasing after of trends or fads has unsettled countless local congregations. If Covenant Theology is either of these, the pursuit of it is a detrimental waste of time. But if it genuinely reflects a biblical understanding of the way God relates, then prayerful implementation is in order.

Many evangelical churches are unaware of Covenant Theology and its wealth of wisdom. The following are guidelines that may be helpful in moving forward in this regard. This is not a recipe to follow given that every congregation is at a unique place of maturity. It is however a series of guidelines that can be shaped, reordered, expanded upon, and prayerfully implemented as the Spirit directs.

KNOW IT

A deepening grasp of the content and issues is crucial. Beyond the obvious reasons of knowing something before it can be taught (which may sometimes not be so obvious!), a deepening knowledge is called for given the tremendous amount of misinformation believed and disseminated regarding Federal Theology. Knowing what it is and what it is not will prove advantageous.

BE MOVED BY LOVE

Christian maturity is to be our pursuit according to Ephesians 3. Such maturity happens when we love (also emphasized in Eph 3). Therefore the desire for the maturity that Covenant Theology can bring to the church must be fueled by love. Keeping this in mind can help curb the pride and arrogance that can easily accompany simply being right. A genuine care for others and for the congregation as a whole can and should be the aim.

KEEP OWEN IN THE OFFICE

Covenant Theology is in the Bible and it can be proven to be so with chapter and verse. Therefore, it is likely most prudent to teach Covenant Theology first and foremost from the divinely inspired Scriptures, the one book that all Christians are obligated to believe. This is not a call for being ignorant of the writings of teachers who have been gifted by the Holy Spirit to help bring maturity to the church. Nor is it a call for hiding gifted teachers from congregations. The church has been blessed by a host of helpful theologians who can and should be called upon at the appropriate time. But instead of winning disciples for the inimitable John Owen or worse, amassing hostility against him, allow him to help in making the Bible clear. To overstate things, consider relegating Owen and company to the office and barring him from the pulpit. In other words, learn from gifted teachers of the past, but focus on allowing them to teach you so that you might teach others more effectively. Introducing select "greats" to others so that they too can appreciate them is commendable, but wisdom regarding where, when, and how often is in order. This writer is not suggesting that appropriate quotations from respectable teachers have no place in sermons. What is being stressed is that selectivity and care will likely serve the church best. Contexts where other teachers can be introduced within the church include theological and historical classes, church conferences, reading groups, and discipleship situations.

CULTIVATE A LOVE FOR *SOLA FIDE*

Dare it be said that if there is a great appreciation for the justifying work of Jesus that comes to sinners by grace alone through faith alone, the soil will be fertile for Covenant Theology? This writer believes so theologically and has witnessed it experientially at the local church level. Where the culture values the doctrine and reality of justification by faith alone, the reasonable next step is for believers to value the work which is nothing shy of the foundation for justification *sola fide*.

MAKE FRIENDS WITH BIBLICAL THEOLOGY

Biblical theology is currently enjoying resurgence in many Christian circles. The evangelical variety of biblical theology is the sort that seeks to show how the whole Bible fits together organically. Unlike liberal forms that sought to undermine the unity of the Bible by attempting to show the differences between Paul's theology, John's theology, and the like, evangelical biblical theology demonstrates the unity within the diversity. Part of the unity is observed in the progress of revelation. With such progress, the storyline unfolds and both the whole and the parts become more and more clear. Such a perspective is a perfect complement to Covenant Theology as it is seen most clearly when both the whole and the individual parts are kept in view as revelation progresses.

Not everyone who contributes to the advancement of biblical theology would consider him or herself covenantal. But their approach compliments Covenant Theology as if they were. This writer proposes that the introduction and utilization of biblical theology and resources stressing its importance will complement and help prepare people for Covenant Theology.

A final thought on biblical theology pertains to children's books. A growing number of books written for small children are essentially biblical theologies for children.[185] They trace the biblical storyline as it unfolds with differing contours and characters while all along following the bigger picture of God's ultimate and eternal purpose coming to fruition in Christ. If churches are not ready for Covenant Theology from the pulpit, then perhaps from the pack and play!

LOVE THE PASTOR

If you are not the pastor and if the pastor is not already the one who is onboard with the theological agenda of implementing Covenant Theology, he is likely priority number one as the one who has the most influential "voice." Several specifics may be helpful here. First, remember to prayerfully approach church leaders with the respect afforded to them by God (Heb 13:17). Second, ask him questions, questions about things that Covenant Theology speaks to,

---

[185] See for example David Helm, *The Big Picture Story Bible* (Wheaton: Crossway, 2014) and Sally Lloyd-Jones, *The Jesus Storybook Bible: Every Story Whispers His Name,* (Grand Rapids: ZonderKidz, 2007).

answers, or relates to. Third, send books or other resources his way. Choose authors he may be most likely to respect. A little research can go a long way here. If he loves John MacArthur for example, direct him toward resources where John affirms the active obedience of Christ or the covenant of redemption.[186] If the pastor is a dispensationalist of the Dallas Seminary type, introduce him to S. Lewis Johnson as someone who affirmed the federal headship of Adam. Fourth, take the pastor to a conference and introduce him to Federal Theology in a different setting where he can have his thinking stimulated and engage in dialogue about such things on different "turf."

DISCIPLE THE LEADERSHIP

A focus on leaders will be vital. The obvious reason for this is because they lead. This means that upon embracing Federal Theology, they will have shared in at least some of the journey, owned it for themselves, and can help in answering questions as well as deal with objections. Such leaders can also fellowship together in weathering the storm if there is one. This can be a lengthy process requiring patience and carefulness. The principles already spelled out above are relevant. Take them to conferences, read with them, utilize authors they will find familiar, and make sure they have long before become vested in the vital nature of justification by grace alone through faith alone in Christ alone. Seeing that justification and therefore the gospel is at stake can make all of the difference in fostering steadfast camaraderie.

---

[186] John MacArthur, "Submission: Heaven's Perspective on the Cross" (Grace to You, September 23, 2013), accessed February 12, 2016, http://www.gty.org/blog/B130923/heavens-perspective-on-the-cross-submission and "Why I Love the Church, Part 3" (Grace to You, no date), accessed February 12, 2016, http://www.gty.org/resources/articles/A352/why-i-love-the-church-part-3

WATCH YOUR MOUTH

One of the most important sensitivities in introducing and implementing the reality of Covenant Theology can be the choice of one's words. There are certain words in this "conversation" that are loaded. Loaded words are those familiar to the family, but potentially confusing if not downright offensive to outsiders. Remembering Christian love can help foster patience here and serve as a restraint in relaxing and opting for family talk. This author is very careful and selective about where and when he uses words that he is relatively certain will confuse and foster anger. The motivation fostered by Christian love can bring patience and the desire to see people mature in understanding even if it is not yet through the language enjoyed by the family so to speak. Examples here include the titles associated with our theological shorthand—covenant of works, covenant of grace, covenant of redemption, and even Covenant Theology.

None of this is denying the place for history and the categories that our Christian ancestors have utilized and found patently helpful. We want everyone to grow in grace and therefore become comfortable in the family.

The implementation of Covenant Theology into the life of a local church that has not enjoyed its richness previously can be challenging to say the least. This chapter has sought to demonstrate that any potential challenge is worth the effort given the great value. To assist with the introduction and implementation the chapter has spelled out a series of instructions that can provide a starting point for prayerful consideration as one approaches the great task of church reform.

- APPENDIX 1 -

THE PROBLEM OF BIBLICISM

If the Bible is the revelation of God whereby he and his will can be truly known, being biblical is the ultimate good. Rightly, Christians have been in pursuit of being biblical since the very start of Christianity. A biblical view of Jesus, the gospel, humanity, the future, etc. have been the admirable pursuit. But is being biblical the same as biblicism?

One's familiarity with how the designation has been used historically will likely have a big influence on the answer. More will be said about this later. The relevance of the question to Covenant Theology is the utilization of words and titles by Covenant Theology to express biblical concepts that are not necessarily themselves the words used in the Bible. The designation "Covenant of Redemption" is a case in point. Used as a kind of shorthand to summarize a biblical reality, the designation could be and sometimes is objected to by some who take a certain kind of biblicist stance.

In the following discussion of biblicism this writer will seek to inform the reader of some of the history of so called biblicism. This will be done in four steps. First, we will see variant usages of biblicism. From self-designations to disparaging labels, divergent use renders biblicism difficult to define. Second, the negative history associated with biblicism will be covered. Third, we will draw upon the negative history and develop arguments for not using the label in any sort of positive light today. Fourth, a better alternative to biblicism will be offered.

USAGE

Biblicism has proven difficult to define, as it is a label used for a range of movements.[187] It has been used positively, negatively, and naively.

SELF DESIGNATION

Some of those who have used the label "biblicist" have done so in order to stress that a theological position or practice has biblical support.[188] Frequently the claim of the biblical position by the biblicist is so in contrast with something traditional, creedal, or ecclesiastical (i.e. "man made").

The label has also been used as a way of defending a theological position that at least appears to be in conflict with another. Someone may say that "I am a biblicist" as a way of responding to would-be accusations of inconsistency or illogic.[189]

PEJORATIVE LABELING

"Biblicist" has been used as a pejorative label fairly often.[190] Basically it is applied negatively to a range of adherents to the Bible.

---

[187] See Erwin Fahlbusch and Geoffrey William Bromiley, *The Encyclopedia of Christianity,* vol. 1, (Grand Rapids: Eerdmans, 1999-2003), 255-56.

[188] Ed Stetzer is an example of an evangelical labeling himself a biblicist. See Ed Stetzer, "Toward a Missional Convention," in *Southern Baptist Identity: An Evangelical Denomination Faces the Future,* ed. David S. Dockery (Wheaton: Crossway, 2009), 201. D. Jeffrey Bingham is an example of a dispensational evangelical who utilizes biblicism positively. See D. Jeffrey Bingham, "Evangelicalism, Dispensationalism, and the Bible," in *Dispensationalism and the History of Redemption: A Developing and Diverse Tradition,* ed. D. Jeffrey Bingham and Glenn R. Kreider (Chicago: Moody, 2015), 48-53.

[189] An example of this would be newly elected President of Calvary Bible College and Seminary, Christopher Cone. See Christopher Cone, "Why I Am Not a Calvinist…Or an Arminian, Part 1," Drcone.com, March 18, 2014, accessed January 2, 2016, http://www.drcone.com/2014/03/18/why-i-am-not-a-calvinistor-an-arminian-part-1/.

[190] A contemporary example can be found in Christian Smith, *The Bible Made Impossible:*

This includes those seen as too strict in subscribing to the Bible, fundamentalists, those who believe in the inspiration of the Bible, and those who minimize systematic or historic theology. Deserved or not, to be branded a biblicist by an adversary is to be seen as somehow subscribing to the Bible in a way that is deemed inappropriate.

NAÏVE CONTEMPORARY USAGE

So is it good or bad to be a biblicist? Contemporary evangelicals who are serious about the inspiration and authority of the Bible may be quick to affirm the title when they hear it. It may be a sort of badge of honor where one says they are being like the Protestant Reformers who heralded *sola scriptura* and rejected humanly contrived traditions. If this is what being a biblicist is, then this writer wants to wear the badge. But as will be shown, history reveals a different story where being a biblicist either by self designation or applied by an antagonist is not at all in line with the Reformation doctrine of *sola scriptura.*

HISTORY

CHRISTOLOGY

One of the greatest controversies in the post-apostolic church concerned the person of Christ. The fourth century Arians denied the deity of Jesus and the followers of Athanasius affirmed that Jesus was not only fully human, but also fully divine. Both groups professed a deep commitment to the inspiration of Scripture. But in an effort to expose the Arian teaching as a denial of what the Scripture meant, extra biblical words were introduced, words to sort

---

Why Biblicism Is Not a Truly Evangelical Reading of Scripture (Ada, MI: Brazos Press, 2011). By "biblicism," Smith means "a theory about the Bible that emphasizes together its exclusive authority, infallibility, perspicuity, self-sufficiency, internal consistency, self-evident meaning, and universal applicability" (viii). For a historical example see David W. Bebbington, *Evangelicalism in Modern Britain: A History from the 1730s to the 1980s*, (New York: Routledge, 1989).

out whether one affirmed the deity of Jesus or not. The Arian sect cried "foul" and they did so as avowed biblicists. As John Piper remarks, "The Arians railed against the unbiblical language being forced on them. They tried to seize the biblical high ground and claim to be the truly biblical people—the pietists, the simple Bible-believers—because they wanted to stay with biblical language only—and by it smuggle in their non-biblical meanings."[191]

TRINITARIANISM

Another noteworthy attack from so-called biblicists took aim at God as Father, Son, and Spirit. This came on the heels of the Protestant Reformation in the sixteenth century. Richard Muller makes some remarkable observations regarding the antitrinitarians of the era. According to Muller, their divergence did not arise from incipient rationalism, but from biblicism. Accordingly, opponents assaulted trinitarianism in the name of being most biblical and correspondingly throwing off the doctrinal restraints imposed by the so-called traditions of men. Their mindset was that the Reformers had not gone far enough in applying *sola scriptura.* Unlike Calvin who saw the value in utilizing extra biblical language to summarize biblical doctrines, especially in the context of combatting heresy, the heretics themselves insisted on only using the wording of the Bible. Muller also points out that it was in the name of supposed "literal exegesis" that the radicals attempted to dismantle traditional trinitarianism and Christology.[192]

---

[191] John Piper, *Contending for Our All: Defending Truth and Treasuring Christ in the Lives of Athanasius, John Owen, and J. Gresham Machen*, (Wheaton: Crossway, 2006), 66.
[192] Richard A. Muller, *Post-Reformation Reformed Dogmatics: The Rise and Development of Reformed Orthodoxy,* Vol. 4: The Triunity of God (Grand Rapids: Baker, 2003), 79. See also pp.19, 62, 99, and 121. Muller says "Virtually all of the sixteenth century antitrinitarians were biblicists" (79).

JUSTIFICATION

Another example of one objecting to what is a biblical teaching in the name of being biblical is Robert Bellarmine (1542-1621). The sixteenth century Roman Catholic counter-reformer vehemently opposed the biblical doctrine of justification by faith alone. He did this by attacking the imputation of Christ's righteousness as something unbiblical. As John Owen notes in the midst of refuting Bellarmine's teachings, "It is usually urged against it, that this imputation of the righteousness of Christ is nowhere mentioned expressly in the Scripture. This is the first objection of Bellarmine against it."[193]

Owen goes on to expose Bellarmine's biblicism as wanting and provides theological conclusions about justification based upon more than what would today amount to simplistic lexical searches.

FANATICISM

The reach of biblicism is not limited to the theological. According to historian Timothy George, some Anabaptists ran naked in the streets because it was supposedly how the Bible told them to behave.[194] Sure enough, Isaiah 20:2-3 says to walk naked and barefoot. So it is therefore biblical to walk around in public while naked and without shoes? For a certain kind of biblicist, the answer is in the affirmative. Thankfully however, many Christians attempt to read texts in a greater context. This leads to more thoughtful inquiry regarding basic interpretive matters such as audience, setting, and history. From that point matters of application in part or in principle can be considered. The one who is most faithful to the text of Scripture is not the one who attempts to find immediate application in every text, especially those describing unique

---

[193] John Owen, *The Doctrine of Justification by Faith* (Monergism Books, 2012), Kindle Electronic Edition: Location 1203-1204.

[194] Timothy George, *Theology of the Reformers* (Nashville: Broadman Press, 1988), 274. He notes that further fanaticism came with some Anabaptists practicing polygamy because it was what a literal hermeneutic rendered.

historical events and figures like the prophet Isaiah in the passage just mentioned.

Theological perspectives such as progressive revelation, the closure of the canon, and the uniqueness of the apostolic era are argued for from the text of Scripture and for those who affirm such things, they then influence the way different biblical texts are read and applied. By largely ignoring these conclusions and their ramifications while instead opting for more of a "let the Bible speak to me directly" approach, the charismatic movement also represents a kind of biblicism.[195]

REASONS BIBLICISM IS A BAD IDEA

IT DOES NOT EXIST

If biblicism is following the Bible alone and therefore insulated from any human influence, tradition, or perspective, it simply does not exist. The fact is that everyone has a theological perspective. Such a perspective may be undeveloped, inconsistent, and uninformed, but it exists. Even when someone says they have "no creed but Christ," are they not professing a creed? Likewise, when someone claims to only follow the Bible and not any theology (suggesting that theology is a human invention), their answer to a simple question like "What do you believe about Jesus?" reveals that they do have a theology.

An interesting case of supposed biblicism that really is not, can been seen in the case of Anabaptist Menno Simons. George explains that Menno brazenly declared that arguments for the Trinity should be limited to "These plain Scriptures, testimonies, and references" and that additional supports were merely "human sophistry and glosses." In summarizing Menno, George goes on to say,

---

[195] As T. S. Caulley observed "From its fundamentalist/biblicist beginning the Pentecostal movement has grown into what is loosely called the charismatic movement, which now touches all of Protestantism…" (T. S. Caulley, "Holy Spirit," in *Evangelical Dictionary of Theology: Second Edition,* ed. Walter A. Elwell, (Grand Rapids: Baker, 2001), 572.

> To go beyond the simple language of the Bible in matters like this was 'like trying to pour the river Rhine or Meuse into a quart bottle.' At the same time we must admit that Menno was not able to stick by his own rule. When he moved from merely quoting traditional proof texts to a description of the deity of Christ and the Holy Spirit, he fell back on terminology which was developed in the history of theology. Christ was called a 'person' by the Church Fathers; the Holy Spirit 'proceeds from the Father through the Son, although he ever remains with God and in God,' and so forth. Nor is this the only instance of Menno's appeal to the wider church tradition.[196]

IT IS NOT BIBLICAL

How is it that biblicism is not biblical? It is not biblical because the Bible itself contains and upholds theological conclusions that have been and are to be affirmed by all Christians. In 1 Timothy 1:15 Paul the Apostle affirms and promotes a theological conclusion and then calls for universal acceptance: "The *saying* is trustworthy and deserving of full acceptance, that Christ Jesus came into the world to save sinners, of whom I am the foremost" (1 Tm 1:15; emphasis added). This is not a quotation from the Old Testament, but a conclusion drawn by Christians regarding the work of Jesus. In more contemporary terms, it is and is to be a confessional statement to which all Christians commonly agree/confess.[197]

The promise of Jesus to lead the disciples "into all the truth" through the coming of "the Spirit of truth" (Jn 16:13) suggests a development of doctrine, specifically doctrinal implications pertaining to Jesus and his gospel. As Carson observes, "Jesus himself is the truth (14:6); now the Spirit of truth leads the disciples into all the implications of the truth, the revelation, intrinsically

---

[196] George, *Theology*, 275.

[197] See George W. Knight, *The Pastoral Epistles: A Commentary on the Greek Text*, New International Greek Testament Commentary (Grand Rapids: Eerdmans, 1992), 99.

bound up with Jesus Christ. There is no other locus of truth; this is *all truth*."[198]

Jesus clearly did not want to leave the disciples to be biblicists so to speak. There were proper conclusions to be drawn and conversely, improper ones.

This maturity by the Spirit's work with the disciples may have ceased with the disciples given their unique place in redemptive history. But the Spirit's work of maturing Christians has been promised to all. Therefore an awareness of the Spirit's work in believers and the church over the centuries seems only reasonable. Unreasonable would be a an expectation that the Holy Spirit has been delaying any real maturity throughout the ages up until *our* arrival on the scene.

IT HAS A SHADY HISTORY

Even if one uses the label "biblicist" in a positive way in an effort to express an earnest desire to affirm biblical doctrines, its history alone makes other choices preferable. As the previous samples demonstrate, some of the most important controversies in the history of Christianity have had the opponents of what is biblical boasting in their biblicism. If for no other reason than this, even the title should be avoided.

IT IS A BREEDING GROUND FOR PERSONALITY CULTS

Pastors and Bible teachers can greatly aid Christians and churches in understanding the Bible and its doctrines. However, apart from adherence to any form of creed or confessional standard serving as guide or boundary, the persuaded listener is subject to the teacher's personal theology whether sound or not. If and when the teacher alters a given theological understanding, followers can expect to either change, live with the conflict, or find another

---

[198] D. A. Carson, *The Gospel According to John*, The Pillar New Testament Commentary (Grand Rapids: Eerdmans, 1991), 539-40; emphasis in original.

individual teacher holding to the position formerly held by the previous teacher. This author has witnessed such a thing happen firsthand with a highly influential evangelical personality who once held an unorthodox view and then changed his view. As he changed, so did many of his followers. Ironically, teacher and follower alike adamantly defended the former position because it was supposedly the biblical position no matter what one might be able to learn from historical theology or systematics. The moral of the story is that the authority was not so much the authority of Scripture, but the popular personality. If the authority would have truly been in the Scripture then the populace would have either not followed the teacher's questionable theological understanding in the first place or they would not have followed him in his change.

IT IS DIVISIVE

The Bible teaches that there is an objective body of Christian doctrine that exists as "the faith" (Jude 3) and as such it is something shared in by believers. It is "a common faith" (Ti 1:4). The biblicist strain (one dare not call it a *tradition)* with its disdain for associating with the historic and traditional, tends to perpetually separate and distance itself from believers from the past, present, and future. To reject historic confessions as anti-biblical inventions of humans is to stand without agreement (i.e. confession).

A possible objection here is that the Bible itself unites and given that the Bible alone is the Word of God, nothing more is needed for true unity among Christians. This sounds good initially until we consider the large number of people who verbalize an affirmation of the Bible as God's Word and then believe and promote doctrines that the Bible itself says disqualify such persons from actually being Christians (e.g. Gal 1).

IT CAN BE AN EXCUSE FOR SLOPPINESS

We are told in the Bible that God's ways are different from ours. This creator/creature distinction coupled with our fallenness provides ample reason to expect some things in Scripture to puzzle us. There is also reason for us to fail in figuring out just how some realities relate to others. A classic case is the exact relationship between divine sovereignty and human responsibility. Yet it is the playing of the "biblicist" card to explain so-called "paradoxes" in the Bible that frequently comes all too fast. Willingness to affirm the veracity of Scripture because one cannot figure out just how two realities relate is commendable if there actually has been thorough investigation of the biblical data in breadth along with the arguments of those who have gone before us. The likelihood of seeing supposed paradoxes diminishes significantly however with a dose of due diligence.

IT IS NOT THE SAME AS *SOLA SCRIPTURA*

The misnomer that the Reformer's doctrine of *sola scriptura* (scripture alone) means that the Bible alone is all we should read, the only authority, or in opposition to tradition is commonly held. But all one needs to do is consult the Reformers themselves to see that they were not calling for opposition to creeds, confessions, or traditions. Champion reformer John Calvin

> ...understood the Reformation not as Scripture versus tradition but as scriptural tradition versus unscriptural tradition. Thoughtful Protestants then, and ever since, have understood the Reformers as arguing for what we might call a tradition that is normed by Scripture. In other words, Protestants know that they use language and conceptual terminology not found explicitly in the Bible; but they understand such are useful in understanding what Scripture says and, at the point where they are found to be inadequate for this task, or even to contradict Scripture, there they must be modified or abandoned. The same is true of the creeds and

> confessions of the church, which are, one might say, the most concentrated deposits of tradition, as affirmed by the church.[199]

One only needs to look as far as Calvin's reliance upon and affirmation of Augustine to see that where tradition was in accordance with Scripture, it was embraced whole-heartedly. *Sola Scriptura* affirms that the Bible is the sole source of special revelation and sole infallible authority. This is markedly different from saying that the Bible is the *only* authority. The Reformers affirmed the former and denied the latter. Biblicism does not stem from *sola scriptura,* but something more like what Keith Mathison describes as *solo scriptura* where no legitimate place is given to the authority of the church.[200]

A BETTER ALTERNATIVE TO BIBLICISM

Making the choice between the supremacy of the Bible and the significance of historic creeds and confessions is a false choice. One can see the Bible alone can be our ultimate authority while simultaneously appreciating the work of God in leading his people by the power of the Spirit in understanding the truth. This is nothing other than what has been called confessional Christianity. Confessional Christianity affirms that the Bible is the ultimate authority and that the Bible's meaning can be known, agreed upon, and wisely summarized in such a way that Christians younger and older can understand well enough to embrace, promote, and defend

[199] Carl R. Trueman, *The Creedal Imperative* (Wheaton: Good News Publishers, 2012), Kindle Electronic Edition: Locations 192-198.

[200] Keith A. Mathison, *The Shape of Sola Scriptura* (Moscow, ID: Canon Press, 2001), 152-153. Mathison demonstrates that what is commonly advocated in evangelicalism in the name of *sola scriptura* simply is not. Rather than being in the tradition of Luther and Calvin, it is akin to their radical opponents. Allen and Swain likewise argue that for the Reformers, "Principled commitment to biblical authority as the ultimate determining factor for all faith and practice did not lead to diminishing concern for ecclesial authority or waning reception of church traditions. Rather *sola Scriptura* aided the course of such reception..." (Michael Allen and Scott R. Swain, *Reformed Catholicity: The Promise of Retrieval for Theology and Biblical Interpretation* [Grand Rapids, MI: Baker Academic, 2015]), 70.

the faith that has once and for all been delivered to the saints (Jude 3).

This confessionalism sees the value of using extra biblical words and categories where necessary. As John Piper wisely observes,

> The truth of biblical language must be vigorously protected with non-biblical language. Bible language can be used to affirm falsehood. Athanasius's experience has proved to be illuminating and helpful in dealing with this fact. Over the years I have seen this misuse of the Bible especially in liberally minded baptistic and pietistic traditions. They use the slogan, "the Bible is our only creed." But in refusing to let explanatory, confessional language clarify what the Bible means, the slogan can be used as a cloak to conceal the fact that Bible language is being used to affirm what is not biblical. This is what Athanasius encountered so insidiously at the Council of Nicaea. The Arians affirmed biblical sentences while denying biblical meaning.[201]

In conclusion it may prove helpful to point out that while not everyone may subscribe to a written understanding of the Christian faith, everyone has one. The conclusion of Carl Trueman on this matter is therefore only sensible:

> I do want to make the point here that Christians are not divided between those who have creeds and confessions and those who do not; rather, they are divided between those who have public creeds and confessions that are written down and exist as public documents, subject to public scrutiny, evaluation, and critique, and those who have private creeds and confessions that are often improvised, unwritten, and thus not open to public scrutiny, not susceptible to evaluation and, crucially and ironically, not,

---

[201] John Piper, *Contending*, 64-65.

> therefore, subject to testing by Scripture to see whether they are true.[202]

Biblicism should be rejected because everyone has a creed even if it is not written down, it is not actually biblical, the history of it is extremely problematic, it is divisive and potentially cultic, and far from what the Reformers meant by *sola scriptura.* A thoughtful confessionalism would instead serve the church well.

[202] Trueman, *Creedal Imperative,* 165-168. See also Samuel Miller's *The Utility and Importance of Creeds and Confessions* (Princeton: D. A. Borrenstein, 1824).

- APPENDIX 2 -

IMPUTATION, JUSTIFICATION, AND THE ACTIVE OBEDIENCE OF CHRIST

In the best spirit of the reformers, informed Protestants eagerly and fittingly echo familiar declarations like Luther's stating that "Faith alone is the doctrine upon which the church stands or falls"[203] or Calvin's describing justification by faith alone as "the main hinge on which religion turns."[204]

Such grand reformational slogans prove timeless given the apostolic pronouncement of condemnation upon any and all *sola fide* rejecters (Galatians 1:8-9), the likes of whom threaten the church in every age.

Indeed justification by grace alone through faith alone in the finished work of Christ alone is a cardinal article of the faith that has once and for all been delivered to the saints.

But from here an important question eventually needs to be raised. If *sola fide* is absolutely foundational to authentic Christianity, what then is foundational to justification by faith alone? Surely the

---

[203] In light of the debate about the actual origin of the quote so often attributed to Luther, there is no doubt it captures his conviction as the following illustrates: "For if the doctrine of justification is lost, the whole of Christian doctrine is lost" (Martin Luther, *Lectures on Galatians* (Saint Louis: Concordia, 1962), 9.

[204] John Calvin, *Institutes of the Christian Religion,* ed. John T. McNeill, trans. Ford Lewis Battles (Louisville: Westminster John Knox, 1960), 3.11.1.

loss of the foundation to the foundation is no less perilous than loss of the *sola fide* foundation. On one level, it could be even more perilous because it may infiltrate the church unawares.

So what is the foundation to the foundation without which justification by faith alone will not stand? In theological parlance, it is the imputation of the perfect righteousness of Christ. This righteousness is Christ's by virtue of his fulfillment of the divine law as the last Adam on behalf of everyone who would ever be justified. In other words, Jesus represented all those who would ever believe unto salvation and in so doing, he fulfilled the righteous requirements of the law of God thereby providing a genuinely righteous basis for God to justify the ungodly. For this to happen, both the so-called active and passive obedience of Jesus is essential (more about this forthcoming).

Recognizing the magnitude of the righteousness of Christ being credited or imputed to the believer as indispensable to the essential truth of justification, Thomas Ascol wisely observes, "If justification is the heart of the gospel, then imputation is the heart of justification."[205] If this is the case then the church must know the truth of imputation, be aware of threats to it, and respond appropriately. In an effort to do this in the pages that follow, we will examine and seek to answer six questions relevant to imputation and the obedience of Christ. The six questions are as follows:

1. *What is the imputation of Christ's righteousness?*
2. *Why does the doctrine of Christ's righteousness matter?*
3. *Who has believed the imputation of Christ's righteousness?*
4. *Where does the Bible teach imputation of Christ's righteousness?*
5. *Who contests the imputation of Christ's righteousness?*
6. *How should the believer respond to the imputation of Christ's righteousness?*

---

[205] Thomas K. Ascol, "Imputation: The Sinners Only Hope," Founders Journal (Winter 2005): 1-13. http://founders.org/fj59/imputation-the-sinners-only-hope/ (accessed on 11.11.11).

WHAT IS THE IMPUTATION OF CHRIST'S RIGHTEOUSNESS?

CHRIST'S RIGHTEOUSNESS IMPUTED

To reiterate in simplest terms, the imputation of the righteousness of Christ is the gracious act of God whereby the righteousness of Christ as the one who fulfilled the divine law is credited to those who believe.[206] This imputing or crediting of righteousness provides the ground upon which God justifies sinners. In other words and in reverse, God justifies sinners even though they utterly lack righteousness while in no way compromising his own righteous law by declaring sinners righteous *based upon a genuine righteousness, namely the righteousness of Jesus.*

This doctrine also answers the Roman Catholic accusation of legal fiction. The forensic act of God declaring sinners righteous (justification) is not based upon a nonexistent and fictitious righteousness, but upon an objectively true and verifiable righteousness, that being the righteousness of Jesus. Such righteousness graciously comes from God in Christ, the last Adam (1 Cor 15:45). As the last Adam, he is the perfect one, not primarily in example, but in representation. Paul says in Romans 5:18, "as one trespass [the trespass of Adam] led to condemnation for all men, so one act of righteousness [one act of righteousness by the last Adam] leads to justification."

John Piper offers this complementary explanation of imputation in his important book *Counted Righteous in Christ: Should We Abandon the Imputation of Christ's Righteousness?:* "By imputation I am referring to

---

[206] The word righteous is a forensic term used of upholding the law. *The Theological Dictionary of the New Testament* utilizes Romans 2:13 and states, "Hence [Paul] can say in R. 2:13: [For it is not the hearers of the law who are righteous before God, but the doers of the law who will be justified]. This follows directly from the fact of the Law. The δίκαιος is the one who as a doer of the Law will be declared righteous by the divine sentence" (*Theological Dictionary of the New Testament*, ed. Gerhard Kittel, Geoffrey W. Bromiley and Gerhard Friedrich, electronic ed., vol.2, [Grand Rapids, MI: Eerdmans, 1964-]), 190. When used in reference to Christ, it is the upholding of the law that is in view as will be seen.

the act in which God counts sinners to be righteousness through their faith in Christ on the basis of Christ's perfect 'blood and righteousness,' specifically the righteousness that Christ accomplished by his perfect obedience in life and death."[207]

CHRIST'S RIGHTEOUSNESS IMPUTED BASED UPON HIS OBEDIENCE

When considering the imputation of Christ's righteousness, it is impossible to keep from discussing the active obedience of Jesus. The two realities are inseparable. The active obedience provides the basis for imputation.

The representative work of Jesus is described as an act of obedience (Rom 5:19). In considering this work, which is ultimately indivisible, theologians throughout the centuries, including Witsius and numerous others who will be cited, have found it helpful to examine Christ's obedience in its two distinct but inseparable aspects—the active and passive.[208] The active is the focus before us as it is most closely associated with Jesus' fulfillment of the positive demands of the law in fulfilling all righteousness (Mt 3:15). Jesus did this as the second Adam so that his righteousness could be imputed to the believing sinner and provide the foundation for justification by faith alone. For justification (the declaration that sinners are righteous) requires more than the removal of guilt by atonement as essential as atonement is. A positive upholding of the law is the required standard of righteousness. The work of Jesus provides both the payment of the law's required penalty as well as fulfillment of the positive demands.

John Murray is helpful in clarifying what has been meant by active and passive obedience. He states that

---

[207] John Piper, Counted Righteous in Christ: Should We Abandon the Imputation of Christ's Righteousness? (Wheaton: Crossway, 2002), 41.
[208] William Stacy Johnson and John H. Leith, ed. *Reformed Reader: A Sourcebook in Christian Theology* (Louisville, KY: Westminster/John Knox Press, 1993), 228, 231-232.

> The real use and purpose of the formula is to emphasize the two distinct aspects of our Lord's vicarious obedience. The truth expressed rests upon the recognition that the law of God has both penal sanctions and positive demands...It is this twofold demand of the law of God which is taken into account when we speak of the active and passive obedience of Christ. Christ as the vicar of his people came under the curse and condemnation due to sin and he also fulfilled the law of God in all its positive requirements. In other words, he took care of the guilt of sin and perfectly fulfilled the demands of righteousness...His obedience becomes the ground of the remission of sin and of actual justification.[209]

To clarify and head off potential objectors at the proverbial pass, Murray explains what is not meant by active and passive obedience. First, passive obedience is not suggesting that anything Christ did was done passively. Everything Christ did was done obediently even as the title passive *obedience* indicates.

A second important clarification is that the distinction between the active and passive obedience is not a distinction of periods. It is our Lord's whole work of obedience in every phase and period that is described as active and passive. So we must avoid the mistake of thinking that the active obedience applies to the obedience of his life and the passive to the obedience of his final sufferings and death.[210] [211]

Charles Hodge assists with further clarification about what is and is not meant:

---

[209] John Murray, *Redemption Accomplished and Applied* (Grand Rapids: Eerdmans, 1955), 22.
[210] Ibid, 20-21.
[211] Lane Tipton offers this similar explanation of the distinction: "Active obedience designates Christ's conformity to the positive precepts of God's moral law in both its Adamic and Mosaic administrations. Passive obedience indicates Christ's bearing of the penal sanctions of the broken law of God in both its Adamic and Mosaic administrations. Active and passive obedience culminate in the exaltation/glorification of the Son of God" (Lane Tipton, "Union with Christ and Justification," in *Justified in Christ*, ed. K. Scott Oliphint, [Scotland: Mentor, 2007]), 24.

> The active and passive obedience of Christ, however, are only different phases or aspects of the same thing. He obeyed in suffering. His highest acts of obedience were rendered in the garden, and upon the cross. Hence this distinction is not so presented in Scripture as though the obedience of Christ answered one purpose, and his sufferings another and a distinct purpose.[212]

WHY DOES THE DOCTRINE OF CHRIST'S IMPUTED RIGHTEOUSNESS MATTER?

This writer was once told that it is okay for a seminary professor to reject the imputation of Christ's righteousness as the ground for justification as long as he does not voice his denial in class very often or make much of an issue of it. Obviously, this person does not think the doctrine matters much. What follows is a four-strand argument for the imputation of Christ's righteousness based upon his perfect law keeping. This argument aims to demonstrate just how much the doctrine of Christ's real righteousness is indispensible to the doctrine of justification.

THE DIVINE LAW REQUIRES RIGHTEOUSNESS [213]

Since the very beginning, God has required human beings to obey him, consequently, this requisite of divine law has never ceased to be the standard. Genesis 2 introduces the reader to the divine requirement imposed upon Adam. The apostle Paul gives further theological clarity on this divine requirement in his development of the formal and informal character of the law in Romans 1-2. Beginning in Romans 1:18 and extending through 2:16, Paul

---

[212] Charles Hodge, *Systematic Theology*, vol. 3, (Oak Harbor, WA: Logos Research Systems, Inc.), 143.

[213] "All error on the subject of Justification springs from the defective views which prevail almost universally among men of the spiritual requirements of God's Law…" James Buchanan, *The Doctrine of Justification: An Outline of its History in the Church and of its Exposition from Scripture* (Amazon Digital Services, 2010), Kindle Electronic Edition: Location 4727-4729.

characterizes this law in terms of God's revelation of himself rendering humans guilty for not honoring him as he desires. God's law is written on tablets of stone and written on the heart, therefore requiring all to live a life of perfect righteousness or face his wrath (see especially 2:12-15).[214] What is God's requirement for acceptance or more specifically, justification? Romans 2:13 says in no uncertain terms that only "the doers of the law…will be justified." This is not a motivational speech given to sinners so they can try harder to make it. Rather Paul is making the point of universal condemnation. For absolutely no one is a "doer of the law" characterized by loving God with heart, soul, mind, and strength.

Therefore, to suggest that sinners can be justified by anything shy of perfect obedience to the law of God is to overlook the immutable divine standard. Obviously, this cannot be accomplished by sinners who are universally condemned for their unrighteousness (Rom 1:18-3:20). The sinner's unrighteous standing is precisely why Scripture underlines the imputation of the righteousness of Christ via his obedience in perfectly keeping the law as the basis for securing justification. To suggest that sinners can be justified apart from the active obedience of Christ would necessitate a relaxing of the divine standard in light of Romans 2:13. But surely God does not relax the standards of his law. For to do so would require that he himself be unjust as judge, a god who compromises his own laws. To the contrary, he magnificently shows himself to be both the just and the justifier of the one who has faith in Jesus (Rom 3:26).

In discussing the doctrine of justification and its inseparable relationship to the requirement of perfect obedience to the law, William Cunningham summarizes the point well in his important contribution to historical theology:

---

[214] When seen as a whole in the context, which includes chapter three, Paul's point is universal condemnation given that absolutely no one other than Christ is righteous (3:10).

> And as there is no perfect righteousness in men themselves to be the ground or basis of their being accepted or admitted to favour and happiness,—as they can no more render perfect obedience than they can satisfy for their sins,—Christ's perfect obedience must become theirs, and be made available for their benefit, as well as His suffering,—His merit as well as His satisfaction.[215]

JUSTIFICATION DEPENDS UPON THE IMPUTATION OF CHRIST'S RIGHTEOUSNESS

Consider this. What is the ground upon which God the righteous can declare the unrighteous to be righteous? It would be scandalous for him to declare sinners righteous based upon anything other than a true righteousness that is provided through a fitting substitute. This is why Reformed theology has been staunchly committed to the imputation of Christ's righteousness received by faith alone as the one and only fitting ground for the believer's justification. For God to simply declare a sinner righteous (apart from the imputation of Christ's obedience to the law) would mean he does not act righteously. He would be justifying the unrighteous based upon something other than a perfect obedience in law keeping, for according to Paul's teaching in Romans 2:13 only "the doers of the law...will be justified." If such an unjust act were done, all of the angels would be compelled to cease in their incessant cries of "holy, holy, holy" (Is 6) as he would be unworthy.

Some suggest that while righteousness is required, it is not the righteousness of Jesus as in the case of his active obedience. Just what kind of righteousness is it then?[216] Does God grant righteousness

---

[215] William Cunningham, *Historical Theology*, vol. 2, (Carlisle: Banner of Truth, 1994), 48.

[216] Obviously this question is used rhetorically here as the righteousness of Christ imputed as the basis for justification is being argued in the paper. But for those today who suggest that the imputed righteousness is a divine attribute or something similar, it would serve them well to at least be informed of the history of such views. John Owen could be a friend in this regard as he invests a great deal in demonstrating how the aforesaid men have been anything but proponents of justification by faith alone in the finished work of Christ alone. See the final section of this paper on rejecters of active obedience for more on this matter.

apart from a human law-keeper representative who is parallel to the human law-breaker representative described in Romans 5? Later in this chapter we will look closer at Romans 5 to demonstrate the biblical nature of Christ's righteousness being the judicial ground for justification. Suffice it to say for now that to have justification by faith alone apart from that which provides the foundation for it to stand is like a legless table suspended in mid air. It simply cannot stand as it depends upon legs to hold it up.

THE IMPUTATION OF CHRIST'S RIGHTEOUSNESS AS THE BASIS FOR JUSTIFICATION IS A CLASSIC PROTESTANT DOCTRINE

The imputed righteousness of Jesus as the basis for justification by faith alone is what John MacArthur describes as "the historic Protestant understanding of justification by faith" in his endorsement of John Piper's book on the subject. Likewise, and in the same place, historian John Hannah states that without the doctrine of the imputed righteousness of Christ "Christianity is not Christian." Piper likewise repeatedly references the doctrine as the historic view held through the ages by those upholding *sola fide.*

THE IMPUTATION OF CHRIST'S RIGHTEOUSNESS IS A BIBLICAL-THEOLOGICAL CONSTRUCT

Some Christian truths are not explicitly stated as such in a single text. Vital doctrines such as the Trinity or the hypostatic union of Christ as God-Man come to mind. We call such realities "Biblical" because they are true expressions of biblical teaching. Yet no solitary verse explicitly states that there is one eternal God who has always and always will be God, existing eternally as Father, Son, and Holy Spirit. Multiple biblical texts are consulted to come to this accurate theological and therefore *biblical* conclusion. So it is with Christ's imputed righteousness. It is an accurate theological conclusion based upon the explicit biblical data. It is therefore what we might call a biblical-theological construct that is truly biblical.

Like many who have rejected the Christian doctrine of the Trinity, some who reject the imputation of Christ's righteousness do so under the moniker of "biblicist." Such was Bellarmine's first objection to imputation observes John Owen in his extensive rebuttal to the Roman Catholic archrival of *sola fide*.[217] Horatius Bonar likewise showed little patience with the biblicism argument in his day and his strong words reflect what was presumably an experiential weariness:

> Rejection of "imputed righteousness" because the words do not actually occur in Scripture, is foolish and weak. Such terms as Christianity, the Trinity, the Eucharist, Plenary Inspiration, are not to be found in the Bible; yet, inasmuch as the thing, or object, or truth which these words truly and accurately cover is there, the term is received as substantially accurate, and made use of without scruple. Such an objection savors more of little-minded caviling than of the truth-seeking simplicity of faith.[218]

Being Biblical is of highest order, but this is far different than the biblicism historically associated with heresy. On a pastoral note, the sooner pastors equip through instruction in matters of theological method, biblicism, and the history of such things, the more stable and productive the church can be.[219]

---

[217] John Owen, *The Doctrine of Justification by Faith* (Monergism Books, 2012), Kindle Electronic Edition: Location 1212. Owen also mentions the heretical Socinians as an example of those who reject biblical realities like the Trinity because the specific word is not used in the Bible (1239).

[218] Horatius Bonar, *The Everlasting Righteousness; Or, How Shall Man Be Just with God?* (Chapel Library, 2013), Kindle Electronic Edition: Location 736-740.

[219] For a fuller treatment of biblicism, see Appendix 1.

WHO HAS BELIEVED THE IMPUTATION OF CHRIST'S RIGHTEOUSNESS

Since both proponents and objectors alike boast in being most biblical (along with most every heretic throughout history!), a glance at the historical landscape via a broad sampling of robust affirmations will at least help with historical perspective in hopefully bringing clarity to who "wears the jersey" so to speak. Given that the two realities of Christ's active obedience and the imputation of his righteousness are inseparable, both will be included.

LUTHER

Alien righteous was the key idea in unlocking the precious truths of genuine Christianity for Martin Luther.[220] This comes out in statements such as, "He has made His righteousness my righteousness, and my sin His sin. If He has made my sin to be His sin, then I do not have it and I am free. If He has made His righteousness my righteousness, then I am righteous now with the same righteousness as He."[221]

CALVIN

No less resolved is Calvin in his promotion and defense of Christ's imputed righteousness as expressed in these words:

> Justified by faith is he who, excluded from the righteousness of works, grasps the righteousness of Christ through faith, and clothed in it, appears in God's sight not as a sinner but as a righteous man. Therefore, we explain justification simply as the acceptance with which God receives us into his favor as righteous men. And we say

[220] See Steven J. Nichols, *Luther, A Life* (Phillipsburg: P&R, 2002), 33.
[221] Martin Luther, "Lectures on Romans," in *Luther's Works,* vol. 25, ed. Hilton C. Oswald, (Saint Louis: Concordia, 1972), 188.

that it consists in the remission of sins and the imputation of Christ's righteousness.[222]

JOHN OWEN[223]

In volume five of his works, John Owen is as ardent as he is clear (albeit verbose!) about both the active and passive obedience of Jesus as well as his righteousness imputed. Here is a sampling: "That which we plead is, that the Lord Christ fulfilled the whole law for us; he did not only undergo the penalty of it due unto our sins, but also yielded that perfect obedience which it did require."[224]

JOHN BUNYAN

If the title of the book *Justification by an Imputed Righteousness or No Way to Heaven but by Jesus Christ* is not adequate in making Bunyan's point (though surely it is!), then the opening proposition removes any ambiguity: "THAT THERE IS NO OTHER WAY FOR SINNERS TO BE JUSTIFIED FROM THE CURSE OF THE LAW IN THE SIGHT OF GOD, THAN BY THE IMPUTATION OF THAT RIGHTEOUSNESS LONG AGO PERFORMED BY, AND STILL RESIDING WITH, THE PERSON OF JESUS CHRIST."[225]

JOHN WESLEY

John Wesley preached a sermon entitled "The Lord Our Righteousness" in 1765. He was adamant in his convictions about the active and passive obedience of Christ along with the imputation of Christ's righteousness.[226]

---

[222] John Calvin, *Institutes of the Christian Religion* (Louisville: John Knox Westminster, 1977), III.xi.2.

[223] For somewhat of a "Cliff's Notes" version of Owen, consult Carl R. Trueman, *John Owen: Reformed Catholic, Renaissance Man,* (Surrey: Ashgate, 2007), 107-113.

[224] John Owen, *Justification,* Kindle Location 5170-5172.

[225] John Bunyan, *Justification by an Imputed Righteousness,* vol. 1 (Bellingham, WA: Logos Research Systems, Inc.), 302.

[226] John Wesley, *Sermons on Several Occasions,* vol. 2 (J&J Harber, 1827), 247. Accessed digitally on 11.25.11 via Google Books. This is not to suggest that Wesley did not also

CONFESSIONS

In addition to individual affirmations, Protestants more collectively have affirmed the active obedience of Jesus. Witness to this can be found in the Westminster Confession (Article 11), the Heidelberg Catechism (HC 60), and the London Baptist Confession of 1689 (Chapter 11).

CONTEMPORARIES

One of the most striking features for this writer about John Piper's defense of imputation in *Counted Righteous* is the endorsement list. The endorsements are as strong as they are diverse, from Arminian Baptist types like Paige Patterson to Calvinists like R. C. Sproul. Even still there are dispensationalists such as John Hannah and Covenantalists like Mike Horton who both affirm a book written by someone who has attempted to distance himself from either such theological vantage points. These alone argue for the veracity of the book's claim to be representative of "the traditional Protestant view."[227]

The imputation of Christ's active obedience as the basis for justification is tied to Jesus fulfilling the law as the last Adam. This is associated with classic Covenant Theology which may cause some to find it odd that those who may otherwise say that they do not affirm Covenant Theology's covenant of works. From this writer's perspective, it is a blessed inconsistency that will hopefully lead some

---

believe other conflicting doctrines that this author finds irreconcilable. For in the same sermon, he says that *faith* is imputed for righteousness. In addition, while Wesley affirmed the doctrine in some sense, his discomfort with the wording and fear that antinomianism could result is noted here by Buchanan: "Wesley's sentiments on this point seem to have been influenced, to some extent, by his fear that the doctrine of imputed righteousness might be perverted into Antinomian error. In his letters to Hervey, he admits the doctrine, but demurs to the phraseology in which it has often been taught; and urges many of the usual objections to it" (Buchanan, *Justification*), Kindle Location 2517-2520.

[227] John Piper, *Counted Righteous*, 53 (cf. p.47 and p.90). Still another endorser of Piper's *Counted Righteous*, Baptist Millard Erickson calls it "the traditional understanding of justification."

to see the vital role that Federal or Covenant Theology plays in upholding imputation and therefore justification *sola fide.*

HISTORY THROUGH HYMNODY

The Protestant church's affirmation and love for Christ who is our righteousness is evident not only in her confessions and gifted spokesmen, but in her musical praise also. It is our pleasure to be reminded in song of Christ our righteousness when we sing words like these:

> *When he shall come with trumpet sound, O may I then in Him be found, Dressed in His righteousness alone, Faultless to stand before the throne.*[228]

> *No condemnation now I dread; Jesus, and all in him, is mine! Alive in him, my living head, And clothed in righteousness divine, Bold I approach the eternal throne, And claim the crown through Christ my own.*[229]

> *I will glory in my Redeemer who crushed the power of sin and death; My only Savior before the holy Judge, the Lamb Who is my righteousness.*[230]

Granted, lyrical samplings are not official statements, but they are definitely indicators of what the church has believed.

PRE-REFORMATION

A comment is likely in order in closing this section on history. Lack of pre-reformation proponents cited may in part be due to this writer's shortcomings as a historian, but are also due to the lack of any such codified doctrine. This does not suggest that the reformers invented it any more so than is true with the developed doctrine of justification by faith alone. D. A. Carson makes just such an apropos comment in saying that "Informed Protestants would not want to

---

[228] *The Solid Rock* by Edward Mote.
[229] *And Can it Be* by Charles Wesley.
[230] I Will Glory in My Redeemer by Steve and Vikki Cook.

say that the Reformation invented their understanding of justification."[231]

WHERE DOES THE BIBLE TEACH THE IMPUTATION OF CHRIST'S RIGHTEOUSNESS?

Given the virtually common confession of Protestantism regarding Christ's imputed righteousness and accompanying active obedience, it is no surprise that biblical support is substantial. Here the focus will be on nine sample texts with some stressing imputation and others active obedience. The comments do not address objections as a focal point. Instead, the primary aim now is citing and explaining the given Scriptures.

2 PETER 1:1

Simeon Peter, a servant and apostle of Jesus Christ, To those who have obtained a faith of equal standing with ours by the righteousness of our God and Savior Jesus Christ (2 Pt 1:1).

The righteousness that brings salvation (salvation described as "a faith" in v.1) is "the righteousness of the God and Savior Jesus Christ."[232] In other words, that which secures salvation and with it an equal standing in salvation is "the righteousness of our God and Savior Jesus Christ." There is not a direct statement calling this

---

[231] D. A. Carson, "The Vindication of Imputation in Justification: On Fields of Discourse and Semantic Fields," in *Justification: What's at Stake in Current Debates*, ed. Mark A. Husbands and Daniel J. Treier (Downers Grove: IVP, 2004), 46.

[232] Some have suggested righteousness here speaks of the fairness of Jesus, but "...righteousness normally refers to the act by which God puts sinners in a right relationship to him. And this seems to be the more likely meaning here...this reference to Christ is in keeping with the whole tenor of the letter, which consistently puts Christ at the same level as God." (Douglas Moo, *2 Peter, Jude*, Grand Rapids: Zondervan, 2011), 35. Similarly, Schreiner states "God's righteousness here does not denote his fairness but his saving righteousness. This accords with the Old Testament, where God's righteousness is parallel to his "salvation" (Pss 22:31; 31:1; 35:24, 28; 40:10; Isa 42:6; 45:8, 13; 51:5–8; Mic 6:5; 7:9)" T.R. Schreiner, *1, 2 Peter, Jude* (electronic ed.). Logos Library System; The New American Commentary (286–287). Nashville: Broadman & Holman Publishers. See also John MacArthur, *2 Peter and Jude* (Chicago: Moody, 2005), 22-23.

imputation per se, but given that it is the righteousness of Christ that brings salvation, any and every Protestant will affirm that it cannot come to the sinner except by imputation. Thus we have Christ's righteousness for the believer unto salvation.

ROMANS 3-4

The third and fourth chapter of Romans has its share of interpretive challenges not limited to matters of imputation. These can be traversed most successfully by allowing the chapters to work together, especially as it relates to chapter four building upon the foundation of three. For example, Romans 4 might give the impression that faith is the actual thing imputed given that a literalist reading says just that—Abraham's "faith is counted as righteousness" (v.5). Some have mistakenly taken this to mean that a person's faith itself is what God imputes as righteousness.[233] But given that chapter four begins with an illustration of Abraham followed by David in order to demonstrate the theological points made in chapter three, credited righteousness is to be seen as coming from actual righteousness, the righteousness from God in Christ discussed in chapter 3. The argument develops from 3:10 where sinners are shown to be completely devoid of any and all righteousness, making justification seemingly impossible (3:20). Hope is signaled in the "But now" statement at 3:21 with the manifestation of "the righteousness of God through faith in Jesus" (3:22). Then in vv.25-26 the work of Christ is said to "show God's righteousness." Again and again such righteousness is said to be for the one who has faith in Jesus (e.g. v.26). The righteousness given belongs to God, is not deserved by sinners, and comes from God to those who believe in Jesus. Therefore "faith, *because of its object*, is imputed to the believer as righteousness."[234] One might say that the

[233] E.g. Robert Gundry who Piper focuses his criticism toward in *Counted Righteous* (15, 44-51, 53-125).
[234] Carson, *Vindication*, 67; emphasis in original.

leaner statements in Romans 4 are like abbreviations given the clearly laid foundation in chapter 3. The complete picture is seen when the chapters are viewed as a unit rather than artificially isolated. This helps safeguard the interpreter from errors due to shortsightedness.

ROMANS 5:18-19

Therefore, as one trespass led to condemnation for all men, so one act of righteousness leads to justification and life for all men. For as by the one man's disobedience the many were made sinners, so by the one man's obedience the many will be made righteous (Rom 5:18–19).

The "one act of righteousness" is the act of Jesus and it "leads to justification." In determining whether or not it is the righteousness of Christ that is imputed to the believer, it is difficult to see how this verse would lead to anything but an affirmative conclusion.

On whether the active or passive righteousness of Christ is in view, Cornelis Venema wisely asserts that

> Christ's obedience upon the cross epitomizes his whole life of obedience. The cross does not exhaust Christ's obedience but reveals it in its most striking form (cf. Phil. 2:8: "becoming obedient to the point of death, even death on a cross"). Indeed were it not for the entirety of Christ's obedience from the beginning to the end of his ministry, it would not be possible to speak of his having died 'the righteous for the unrighteous, that he might bring us to God' (1 Pet. 3:18). Even though the reference to the 'one act of righteousness' in Romans 5 describes Christ's death upon the cross, it is not possible to separate this act of obedience from his entire life 'under the law' (cf. Gal. 4:4).[235]

[235] Cornelis P. Venema, *The Gospel of Free Acceptance in Christ*, (Carlisle: Banner of Truth Trust, 2006), 240.

And Horatius Bonar highlights that "The imputation of the first Adam's sin to us, and of the last Adam's righteousness, are thus placed side by side. The transference of our guilt to the Divine Substitute, and the transference of that Substitute's righteousness or perfection to us, must stand or fall together."[236] [237]

ROMANS 10:4

Brothers, my heart's desire and prayer to God for them is that they may be saved. For I bear them witness that they have a zeal for God, but not according to knowledge. For, being ignorant of the righteousness of God, and seeking to establish their own, they did not submit to God's righteousness. For Christ is the end of the law for righteousness to everyone who believes (Rom 10:1–4).

The sort of righteousness that is needed in order to be "saved" (v.2) is "the righteousness of God" or "God's righteousness" (vv.2-3). Such a righteousness cannot come through sinners attempting to obey the law, rather Christ is "the culmination of the law, so that there might be righteousness for everyone who believes" (Doug Moo's rendering).[238] Worded differently, but capturing the same textual intent is this rendering: "For the end (or goal or consummation) of the law [is] *Christ for righteousness* to everyone who believes."[239]

So it is Christ's work in relation to the law and its fulfillment that brings righteousness for everyone who believes. It is *Christ for righteousness*! And the object of faith given the immediate and broader context of Romans 10 (see especially vv.10-14) is Christ. Therefore, it is the righteousness of God in the person of Jesus that is received upon believing and therefore completely appropriate to refer to the righteousness being the righteousness of Christ.

---

[236] Horatius Bonar, *Everlasting Righteousness,* Kindle Location 704-706.
[237] See also John Owen, *Justification,* Kindle Location 850-855. He definitively says "this is the righteousness of Christ, *even his obedience*" (emphasis added).
[238] Douglas Moo, *The Epistle to the Romans* (Grand Rapids: Eerdmans, 1996), 630.
[239] Piper, *Counted Righteous,* 87; emphasis added.

2 CORINTHIANS 5:21

The Apostle Paul explains the work of Jesus for sinners by saying, "For our sake he made him to be sin who knew no sin, so that in him we might become the righteousness of God" (2 Cor 5:21). Commenting on 5:19-21, Carson says,

> The thought that our sins are imputed to Christ commends itself as a parallel to the notion that righteousness is in turn imputed to us. What might be thought by some to stand against such a view is that this righteousness is explicitly said to be *God's* righteousness, not *Christ's* righteousness…but even so the opening clause of verse 19 must not be overlooked: *God was in Christ* reconciling the world to himself, or *"God* was reconciling the world to himself in *Christ.*"[240]

And albeit on a more popular level, John MacArthur, captures the biblical-theological intent of the passage with this summary: "Our iniquitous life was legally charged to Him on the cross, as if He had lived it, so that His righteous life could be credited to us, as if we lived it. That is the doctrine of justification by imputation—the high point of the gospel."[241]

PHILIPPIANS 3:8-9

Indeed, I count everything as loss because of the surpassing worth of knowing Christ Jesus my Lord. For his sake I have suffered the loss of all things and count them as rubbish, in order that I may gain Christ and be found in him, not having a righteousness of my own that comes from the law, but that which comes through faith in Christ, the righteousness from God that depends on faith (Phil 3:8–9).

So the appropriate kind of righteousness, the kind that saves is "a righteousness…which comes through faith in Christ, the

---

[240] Carson, *Vindication*, 69-70; emphasis in original.
[241] John MacArthur, *2 Corinthians* (Chicago: Moody, 2003), 217.

righteousness from God that depends on faith" (v.9). Does Christ then, being the object of faith, equate to the righteousness in view being Christ's righteousness? The text does not explicitly name it to be Christ's. But it is the most natural way of understanding righteousness that is required by God of human beings given that Jesus is the incarnate one for our benefit and more specifically as the last Adam (1 Corinthians 15:45). For Jesus to be the representative who humbles himself, becomes a human being, obeys the law of God as a human being, and does so even to the point of death on a cross is most naturally understood in terms of Christ being the believer's righteousness for justification. The emphasis in the text on Jesus makes this the most fitting conclusion. For the righteousness to be based upon something other than the work of Jesus ignores the overwhelming emphasis in the passage on Jesus.

Why then is it called a righteousness from God? The answer given by Francis Turretin in the 1600s would be difficult to improve upon: "This is called the righteousness of God because it belongs to a divine person and so is of infinite value and is highly pleasing and acceptable to God. By this righteousness then, we understand the entire obedience of Christ—of his life as well as of his death, active as well as passive."[242]

1 CORINTHIANS 1:30

And because of him you are in Christ Jesus, who became to us wisdom from God, righteousness and sanctification and redemption (1 Cor 1:30).

With measured sarcasm, D. A. Carson concludes that "it is surely a brave scholar who insists that 'Christ has become...our righteousness' has nothing to do with Christ's righteousness being imputed to us."[243] According to divine monergistic grace, the sinner

[242] Francis Turretin, *Justification* (Phillipsburg: P&R 2004), 35.
[243] Carson, *Vindication*, 76.

is "in Christ Jesus" and Jesus, by virtue of our being in union with him, "became to us…righteousness."

GALATIANS 4:4-5

But when the fullness of time had come, God sent forth his Son, born of woman, born under the law, to redeem those who were under the law, so that we might receive adoption as sons (Gal 4:4–5).

Lloyd-Jones does us a service in weaving multiple important texts together to present Galatians 4 in relation to Jesus who came under the law as the one who would in fact fulfill it. He notes,

> Ah yes, but in His life He gave an active obedience. Paul says, 'When the fulness of the time was come, God sent forth his Son, made of a woman, made under the law, to redeem them that were under the law' (Gal. 4:4–5). And this is how He did it: He rendered a perfect obedience to the law. He kept it fully. He carried it out in every jot and tittle. He said He was going to do it: 'Think not that I am come to destroy the law, or the prophets: I am not come to destroy, but to fulfil' (Matt. 5:17). And as we have seen, 'One jot or one tittle shall in no wise pass from the law, till all be fulfilled' (Matt. 5:18). And He did so. He kept the law perfectly.[244]

PHILIPPIANS 2:8

And being found in human form, he humbled himself by becoming obedient to the point of death, even death on a cross (Phil 2:8).

Jesus was obedient to the point of death, even death on a cross. This does not say or suggest that the crucifixion was the one and only act of obedience. More appropriately it is the consummation rather than the totality as it is *"to the point of death,* even death on a cross" (2:8). The emphasis in Philippians 2 is the humility of Jesus

---

[244] David Martin Lloyd-Jones, *God the Father, God the Son,* (Wheaton: Crossway Books, 1996), 336.

and his humility was not limited to his death. For as the previous verses indicate, his incarnation and subsequent life demonstrate humble submission (read obedience, even vicarious obedience as it is an obedience for others). His life was lived in submission to the will of God (Jn 4:34, 5:30, 6:38) and he did nothing less than obediently submit to the will of God in fulfilling the law of God (Mt 5:17).[245]

The biblical data is the driving force leading one to embrace the reality of Christ's active obedience to the divine law and corresponding imputed righteousness as the foundation for justification by faith alone.

WHO CONTESTS THE IMPUTATION OF CHRIST'S RIGHTEOUSNESS?

Rejection of the imputation of Christ's righteousness has quite a history, though not one that is friendly to the gospel.

ROME

The Roman Catholic foundational doctrine of synergistic justification calls for her beloved infused righteousness and corresponding rejection of Christ's imputed righteousness by faith alone. There is nothing puzzling about this. Rome rejects imputation in the sense put forth in this paper because she rejects the Protestant monergistic doctrine of *sola fide.*[246]

What *is* puzzling, however, is the unusual position of those professing to be Protestant while at the same time rejecting the foundation of *sola fide* which is imputed righteousness, the righteousness of Christ via his active and passive obedience

[245] Essential to the Son fulfilling the law is his learning obedience (Hebrews 5:8).

[246] See *The Council of Trent, Session VI, Canon 11* which states: "If anyone says that men are justified either by the sole imputation of the justice of Christ or by the sole remission of sins, to the exclusion of the grace and the charity which is poured forth in their hearts by the Holy Ghost, and remains in them, or also that the grace by which we are justified is only the good will of God, let him be anathema" (http://www.ewtn.com/library/councils/trent6.htm), accessed January 2, 2016.

regarding the law of God. This is why Buchanan comments, "Indeed, most of the objections which have been urged against the doctrine of imputed righteousness, by those who admit a vicarious satisfaction for sin, have been derived from Popish or Socinian sources, and bear a striking resemblance to those which Bellarmine and Crellius employed in a former age."[247]

ANDREAS OSIANDER

Osiander (1498-1522) is infamous for his rejection of the doctrine in view and resultant label of "heretic" in Owen's volume on justification. Particularly troubling was his teaching that "the righteousness by which we are justified is the eternal righteousness of God."[248]

Do individuals living today who say similar things in an effort to keep from embracing Christ's imputed righteousness, realize it is not a new conclusion they have come upon and that the alignment is not a favorable one? In some ways we can hope not and in other ways one would like to think that teachers know something about historical associations.[249]

---

[247] Buchanan, *Justification,* Kindle Location 4489-4494.

[248] Ibid, Kindle Location 2198-2203. Francis Turretin also addressed the error of Osiander. Turretin writes, "However, there is no need to remark that by the righteousness of Christ we do not understand here the 'essential righteousness of God' dwelling in us…That righteousness could not be communicated to us subjectively and formally which is an essential attribute of God without our becoming gods also. And the Scripture everywhere refers the righteousness of Christ, which is imputed to us, to be the obedience of his life and the suffering of his death, by which he answered the demands of the law and perfectly fulfilled it" (Francis Turretin, *Institutes of Elenctic Theology,* vol. 2, *First Through Tenth Topics,* ed. James T. Dennison Jr, trans. George Musgrave Giger, Phillipsburg, NJ: P & R Publishing, 1992), 650.

[249] See Andrew V. Snider, "Justification and the Active Obedience of Christ: Toward a Biblical Understanding of Imputed Righteousness" (ThM thesis, Master's Seminary, 2002). Snider, like other opponents of Reformed theology before him, says "It is the divine righteousness, that perfect harmony with God's character and standard which is the attribute of the Godhead, that is imputed to the believer" 96-97. For a rebuttal to Snider see Peter Christopher Sammons, "No Hope Without It!: The Doctrine of Active Obedience Defined and Vindicated" (ThM thesis, Master's Seminary, 2013).

GOVERNMENTALISTS

A denial of the active obedience of Christ in 17th century America was associated with the governmental theory of the atonement that denied the penal substitutionary doctrine of the atonement as well as imputed righteousness. The denial of substitution by the likes of Grotius (1583-1645) and Charles Finney (1792-1875) eliminated the need for the imputation of Christ's righteousness and active obedience.[250]

NEW PERSPECTIVES, WRIGHT, FEDERAL VISION, AND NORMAN SHEPHERD

A common element among numerous individuals and/or movements including the New Perspectives, N.T. Wright, Norman Shepherd, and the Federal Vision that are on "the radar" for their deviating compromises pertaining to *sola fide* is a rejection of the imputed righteousness of Christ.[251] [252]

SELECT DISPENSATIONALISTS

Some dispensationalists like Darby reject the active obedience of Christ and the imputation of Christ's righteousness in fulfilling the law. But neither is uniformly rejected by dispensationalists as evidenced in the clear emphasis by someone like John MacArthur.

---

[250] Louis Berkhof, The History of Christian Doctrines (Carlisle: Banner of Truth, 1969), 195-6. See also Charles Grandison Finney, Lectures on Systematic Theology: Embracing Moral Government, the Atonement, Moral and Physical Depravity, Natural, Moral, and Gracious Ability, Repentance, Faith, Justification, Sanctification, &c, (London: William Tegg and Co., 1851), 330-337.

[251] This point is well made by David VanDrunen at the conclusion of his helpful analysis "Where We Are: Justification Under Fire in the Contemporary Scene" in *Covenant, Justification, and Pastoral Ministry: Essays by the Faculty of Westminster Seminary California*, ed. R. Scott Clark (Phillipsburg: P&R, 2007), 55.

[252] Evaluation of the New Perspectives on Paul has been done and done well on multiple occasions so as to not need yet another critique here. E.g. Guy Prentiss Waters, *Justification And The New Perspectives On Paul: A Review And Response* (Phillipsburg: P&R, 2004). For a more up to date critique that includes some constructive criticism of Piper, see Michael S. Horton, "Engaging N.T. Wright and John Piper" in *Justified: Modern Reformation Essays on the Doctrine of Justification*, ed. Ryan Glomsrud and Michael S. Horton, (Escondido: Modern Reformation, 2010), 11-32.

References to the active obedience of Christ by MacArthur are common (e.g. the *MacArthur Study Bible*, commentaries, and sermons) and he is not shy to equate it with the gospel as seen in his comments on 2 Corinthians 5 cited earlier. Other dispensationalists like John Hannah likewise associate it with genuine Christianity. Long time professor at Dallas Theological Seminary, S. Lewis Johnson was a staunch promoter and defender of the doctrine.

As to why other dispensationalists reject the doctrines, this writer suspects it is primarily out of the desire to avoid association with the federal headship of Adam. Disconcertingly, those dispensationalists who reject the active obedience of Christ as the basis for imputed righteousness fail to see that *sola fide* cannot stand without it. Put another way, they are living on borrowed equity. This may work for a time, but without a legitimate foundation (imputed righteousness through Christ's active obedience), their Protestant doctrine of justification is vulnerable to say the least.

Darby's vehement opposition to the imputation of Christ's righteousness and therefore his active obedience appears to stem from his perspective on the law. The following two quotations are worth hearing:

> My adversaries say it was Christ's keeping the law for us; but when I ask for scripture, it is impossible to have any. It is a mistake to say "Brethren" deny Christ's righteousness. Of course, personally, He was righteous. They deny the imputation of His law-keeping to the believer, and that the righteousness of God means anything of the kind.[253]

> The last question, which lies behind all this is, Why is the believer accounted righteous? My adversaries say it is because Christ kept the law in his stead, and that this is imputed to him. I deny this as

[253] Collected Writings of J.N. Darby: Doctrinal 3. http://bibletruthpublishers.com/collected-writings-of-j-n-darby-doctrinal-3/lbd15235 (accessed December 4, 2015).

> an utterly anti-scriptural doctrine; I have said it and repeat it. I know many beloved and godly' souls have been so taught, and have held it in integrity of heart. But since it is insisted on, and the truth is evil spoken of, I speak more plainly. It is an anti-scriptural doctrine which does great injury to souls.[254]

In viewing law as practically Israel specific, it made no sense for Darby to have Jesus fulfilling the law for people who had no obligation to law whatsoever. Such a perspective fails to take into account that the moral law of God applies to all human beings as it is written on the heart (Rom 2:15), that to have no law would be to have no such thing as sin given that "sin is lawlessness" (1 Jn 3:4), and that justification could not even exist apart from the existence of law as it is the legal declaration of righteousness which is itself inseparably associated with law.

Therefore it would seem that the doctrines of Darby, in so far as they undermine the foundation for justification, are the real culprit in bringing "great injury to souls" (to use his words).[255]

NEW COVENANT THEOLOGY

The movement known as New Covenant Theology has distanced itself from both Dispensationalism and Covenant Theology. But more like some dispensationalists, they have rejected the active obedience of Christ. Objections by New Covenant writers appear to be restatements of former objections including but not limited to a phobia of anything remotely resembling a covenant obligation with Adam. But given the common connection between disregarding imputation and being confused about the gospel, the trajectory for those who still hold to *sola fide* but reject active obedience and Christ's imputed righteousness does not look favorable.

---

[254] Ibid.

[255] The hostility of Darby toward the imputation of Christ as law keeper sheds light on why those associated with the Brethren movement follow suit.

More recent developments in New Covenant Theology have led to some of its proponents affirming, articulating, and defending the active obedience of Christ. This is a welcome change to a new and evolving theological school.[256]

HOW SHOULD ONE RESPOND TO THE IMPUTATION OF CHRIST'S RIGHTEOUSNESS?

With unrivaled pastoral eloquence and persuasion, Charles Spurgeon presses all to see the absolute need for perfect righteousness:

> Man must have a righteousness, or God cannot accept him. Man must have a perfect obedience, or else God cannot reward him. Should He give Heaven to a soul that has not perfectly kept the Law? That were to give the reward where the service is not done, and that before God would be an act which might impeach His Justice. Where, then, is the righteousness with which the pardoned man shall be completely covered, so that God can regard him as having kept the Law, and reward him for so doing? Surely, my Brothers and Sisters, none of you are so drunk as to think that this righteousness can be worked out by yourselves! You must despair of ever being able to keep the Law perfectly.[257]

But despair is not the only option if there is perfect righteousness available to the sinner. Such righteousness compels Spurgeon to continue saying,

---

[256] See Kingdom Through Covenant: A Biblical-Theological Understanding of the Covenants (Wheaton: Crossway, 2012) by Peter Gentry and Stephen Wellum, 663-672.

[257] Metropolitan Tabernacle Pulpit JEHOVAH TSIDKENU THE LORD OUR RIGHTEOUSNESS NO. 395, A SERMON DELIVERED ON SUNDAY MORNING, JUNE 2, 1861, BY REV. C. H. SPURGEON, AT THE METROPOLITAN TABERNACLE, NEWINGTON. http://www.spurgeongems.org/vols7-9/chs395.pdf (accessed October 30, 2015).

> We must believe, then—for there is no other alternative—that the Righteousness in which we must be clothed, and through which we must be accepted, and by which we are made meet to inherit eternal life, can be no other than the work of Jesus Christ! We, therefore, assert—believing that Scripture fully warrants us—that the life of Christ constitutes the Righteousness in which His people are to be clothed. His death washed away their sins, His life covered them from head to foot; His death was the Sacrifice to God, His life was the gift to man, by which man satisfies the demands of the Law. Herein the Law is honored, and the soul is accepted![258]

Returning to the notion of a professor who rejects the imputation of Christ's righteousness and correspondingly Christ's active obedience, maybe the true scandal is not so much in what he rejects, but in his inability to regularly as well as jubilantly proclaim the crucial and glorious doctrine of Christ our righteousness! For apparently his hope *is not* built on Jesus' blood *and righteousness* (to borrow from Zinzendorf's hymnody).

What would motivate a professing Protestant to reject a doctrine that is traditional to Protestantism? Furthermore, what would prompt one to abandon the doctrine of Christ's imputed righteousness when such an action is repeatedly associated with teachers and movements who likewise repudiate justification by faith alone in the classic sense?

This writer is moved to wholeheartedly affirm as well as joyfully proclaim the biblical and likewise historic Protestant doctrine of the imputed righteousness of Jesus. It is only such a righteousness that can meet the requirement of the God who declares "You therefore must be perfect, as your heavenly Father is perfect" (Mt 5:48). Given this standard, no other righteousness will do in securing justification other than Christ's perfect righteousness.

---

[258] ibid.

- BIBLIOGRAPHY -

Akin, Daniel L. *1, 2, 3 John.* Nashville: Broadman & Holman, 2001.

Alexander, Joseph Addison A, Merrill F Unger, and John Eadie. *Commentary on Isaiah.* Grand Rapids: Kregel Publications, 1992.

Allen, Michael R. *Justification and the Gospel: Understanding the Contexts and Controversies.* Grand Rapids: Baker, 2013.

Allen, Michael and Scott R. Swain. *Reformed Catholicity: The Promise of Retrieval for Theology and Biblical Interpretation.* Grand Rapids, MI: Baker Academic, 2015.

Allison, Gregg R. *Historical Theology: An Introduction to Christian Doctrine.* Grand Rapids: Zondervan, 2011.

Archer, Gleason L., Laird R. Harris, and Bruce K. Waltke. *Theological Wordbook of the Old Testament.* Chicago: Moody, 1980.

Ascol, Thomas. 'Imputation: The Sinner's Only Hope.' Last modified 2016. Accessed December 12, 2015. http://founders.org/fj59/imputation-the-sinners-only-hope/.

Bahnsen, Greg L., Walter C. Kaiser, Douglas J. Moo, and Wayne G. Strickland. *Five Views on Law and Gospel.* Edited by Stanley N. Gundry. Grand Rapids: Zondervan, 1996.

Balz, Horst, and Gerhard Schneider, eds. *Exegetical Dictionary of the New Testament.* Edited by Gerhard Schneider. Grand Rapids: Eerdmans, 1994.

Barth, Karl. *Church Dogmatics*, 14 vols., eds. G. W. Bromiley, T. F. Torrance. Edinburgh: T&T Clark, 2010, IV/1.

Bebbington, David W. *Evangelicalism in Modern Britain A History from the 1730s to the 1980s.* New York: Routledge, 1989.

Benjamin Breckinridge Warfield. *Selected Shorter Writings 2 Vol.* Edited by John Meeter. Phillipsburg: P&R Publishing, 2001.

Berkhof, Louis. *History of Christian Doctrine*. Carlisle: Banner of Truth, 1969.

______. *Systematic Theology*. Grand Rapids: Eerdmans, 1978.

Bingham, D. Jeffrey. "Evangelicalism, Dispensationalism, and the Bible," in *Dispensationalism and the History of Redemption: A Developing and Diverse Tradition*, eds. D. Jeffrey Bingham and Glenn R. Kreider. Chicago: Moody, 2015.

Bolt, John, and Herman Bavinck, eds. *Reformed Dogmatics*. Grand Rapids: Baker Academic, 2011.

Bonar, Horatius. *The Everlasting Righteousness: How Shall Man Be Just with God?* Edinburgh: Banner of Truth, 1993.

Boyce, J.P. 'Boyce's Abstract of Systematic Theology–Chapter 22.' Last modified 2016. Accessed December 12, 2015. http://founders.org/library/boyce1/ch22/.

Brand, Chad, and Archie England. *Holman Illustrated Bible Dictionary*. Edited by Charles W. Draper. Nashville: Broadman & Holman, 2003.

Buchanan, James. *The Doctrine of Justification: An Outline of Its History in the Church, and of Its Exposition from Scripture. With Special Reference to Recent Attacks on the Theology of the Reformation. The Second Series of the 'Cunningham Lectures'.* Grand Rapids: Baker, 1978.

Bunyan, John. *The Works of John Bunyan, Volumes 1-3*. Mulberry, IN: Sovereign Grace Publishers, 2001.

Calvin, John. *Commentary on Romans.* Christian Classics Ethereal Library. Accessed December 12, 2015. http://www.ccel.org/ccel/calvin/calcom38.vi.iii.html.

______. *Institutes of the Christian Religion by John Calvin*. United States: Logos Research Systems, 1998.

Carson, D. A. *The Pillar New Testament Commentary: The Gospel according to John*. Grand Rapids: Eerdmans, 1991.

'Catechism of the Catholic Church - Grace and Justification.' Last modified 2016. Accessed December 12, 2015. http://www.vatican.va/archive/ccc_css/archive/catechism/p3s1c3a2.htm.

Chafer, Lewis Sperry. *Systematic Theology*. Dallas, TX: Dallas Theological Seminary Press, 1948.

Chalke, Steve and Alan Mann, *The Lost Message of Jesus.* Grand Rapids: Zondervan, 2003.

Charnock, Stephen. *Works of Stephen Charnock*. Mulberry, IN: Sovereign Grace Publishers, 2001.

Cheeseman, John. et al., *The Grace of God in the Gospel,* Carlisle: Banner of Truth, 1972.

Clark, R. Scott "A Brief History of Covenant Theology," accessed December 31, 2015, http://spindleworks.com/library/CR/clark.htm.

______, *Caspar Olevian and the Substance of the Covenant: The Double Benefit of Christ.* Grand Rapids: Reformation Heritage Books, 2006.

______, ed. *Covenant, Justification, and Pastoral Ministry: Essays by the Faculty of Westminster Seminary California*. Phillipsburg: P&R Publishing, 2007.

Colquhoun, John. *A Treatise on the Law and the Gospel.* Morgan, PA: Soli Deo Gloria Publications, 1999.

Cone, Christopher. "Why I Am Not a Calvinist…Or an Arminian, Part 1," Drcone.com, March 18, 2014, accessed January 2, 2016, http://www.drcone.com/2014/03/18/why-i-am-not-a-calvinistor-an-arminian-part-1/.

Couch, Mal. *An Introduction to Classical Evangelical Hermeneutics: A Guide to the History and Practice of Biblical Interpretation*. 2nd ed. Grand Rapids: Kregel, 2000.

Crossway Books. *The Holy Bible English Standard Version*. Wheaton: Crossway, 2002.

Cunningham, William. *Historical Theology: A Review of the Principal Doctrinal Discussions in the Christian Church since the Apostolic Age*. Edinburgh: Banner of Truth, 1960.

Darby, John Nelson. 'The Collected Writings of J.N. Darby.' Accessed December 12, 2015. http://bibletruthpublishers.com/collected-writings-of-j-n-darby-doctrinal-3/lbd15235.

Duncan, J. Ligon. "History of Covenant Theology" (sermon, First Presbyterian Church, Jackson, MS, September 3, 1998), accessed December 31, 2015, http://www.fpcjackson.org/resource-library/classes-and-training/history-of-covenant-theology

______. *Introduction to Covenant Theology*. Charlotte, NC: Reformed Theological Seminary, 2014).

Elam, Andrew M, Robert C Van Kooten, and Randall A Bergquist. *Merit and Moses: A Critique of the Klinean Doctrine of Republication*. Eugene: Wipf & Stock Publishers, 2014.

Elwell, Walter A., ed. *Evangelical Dictionary of Theology*. Grand Rapids: Baker, 1995.

Enns, Paul P. *The Moody Handbook of Theology*. Chicago: Moody, 1989.

Erickson, Millard J. *Christian Theology*. 2nd ed. Grand Rapids: Revell, a division of Baker Publishing Group, 1986.

Estelle, Bryan D., J. V. Fesko, and David VanDrunen. *The Law Is Not of Faith: Essays on Works and Grace in the Mosaic Covenant*. Phillipsburg: P&R Publishing, 2009.

Fahlbusch, Erwin, and Geoffrey W. Bromiley. *The Encyclopedia of Christianity: Vol. 1*. Grand Rapids: Eerdmans, 2003.

Feinberg, John S. *Continuity and Discontinuity: Perspectives on the Relationship between the Old and New Testaments: Essays in Honor of S. Lewis Johnson, Jr*. Wheaton: Crossway, 1988.

Fesko, J. V. *The Covenant of Redemption: Origins, Development, and Reception*. Göttingen, Germany: Vandenhoeck & Ruprecht, 2016.

______. *The Theology of the Westminster Standards: Historical Context and Theological Insights*. Wheaton: Crossway, 2014.

______. *Justification: Understanding the Classic Reformed Doctrine*. Phillipsburg: P&R Publishing, 2008.

Finney, Charles Grandison. *Lectures on Systematic Theology: Embracing Moral Government, the Atonement, Moral and Physical Depravity, Natural, Moral, and Gracious Ability, Repentance, Faith, Justification, Sanctification, &c.* London: William Tegg and Co., 1851.

Fisher, Edward, and Fisher Edward. *The Marrow of Modern Divinity*. Ross-shire, Scotland: Christian Focus Publications, 2009.

Flavel, John. *The Works of John Flavel: 6 Volume Set*. Edinburgh: The Banner of Truth Trust, 1997.

Fruchtenbaum, Arnold. 'The Eight Covenants of the Bible.' Accessed December 12, 2015. http://www.messianicassociation.org/ezine17-af.covenants.htm.

Fuller, Daniel P. *The Unity of the Bible: Unfolding God's Plan for Humanity*. Grand Rapids: Zondervan, 1997.

______. *Gospel and Law: Contrast or Continuum - the Hermeneutics of Dispensationalism and Covenant Theology*. Grand Rapids: Eerdmans, 1980.

Gaffin, Richard B. *Resurrection and Redemption: A Study in Paul's Soteriology*. 2nd ed. Phillipsburg: P&R Publishing, 1987.

______. *By Faith, Not by Sight: Paul and the Order of Salvation*. 2nd ed. Phillipsburg: P&R Publishing, 2013.

Garrett, Duane A., and P. Ferris. *Hosea, Joel (New American Commentary)*. Nashville: Broadman & Holman Publishers, 1997.

Gentry, Peter J., and Stephen J. Wellum. *Kingdom through Covenant: A Biblical-Theological Understanding of the Covenants*. Wheaton: Crossway, 2012.

George, Timothy F. *Theology of the Reformers*. Nashville: Broadman & Holman Publishers, 1988.

Gibson, David and Jonathan Gibson, ed. *From Heaven He Came and Sought Her: Definite Atonement in Historical, Biblical, Theological, and Pastoral Perspective*. Wheaton: Crossway, 2013.

Gillespie, Patrick. *The Ark of the Covenant Opened, or, A Treatise of the Covenant of Redemption Between God and Christ, as the Foundation of the Covenant of Grace.* London: Thomas Parkhurst, 1677.

Glomsrud, Ryan, and Michael S. Horton, eds. *Justified: Modern Reformation Essays on the Doctrine of Justification*. Escondido: Modern Reformation, 2010.

Goldsworthy, Graeme. *Gospel-Centered Hermeneutics: Foundations and Principles of Evangelical Biblical Interpretation*. Downers Grove: Inter-Varsity Press, 2010.

Grudem, Wayne A. *Systematic Theology: An Introduction to Biblical Doctrine*. Grand Rapids: Zondervan, 1994.

Hart, D. G. *Between the Times: The Orthodox Presbyterian Church in Transition, 1945-1990.* Willow Grove, PA: Committee for the Historian of the Orthodox Presbyterian Church, 2011.

Helm, David R. *The Big Picture Story Bible*. 2nd ed. Wheaton: Crossway, 2010.

Hendriksen, William. *Exposition of the Gospel According to Luke.* Grand Rapids: Baker Book House, 1953.

Hodge, Charles. *A Commentary on Romans*. Carlisle, PA: Banner of Truth, 1989.

______. *Ephesians* (Wheaton: Crossway, 1994), 30.

______. *Systematic Theology, Volumes 1-3.* Peabody, MA: Hendrickson Publishers, 1981.

Horton, Michael S. *The Christian Faith: A Systematic Theology for Pilgrims on the Way*. Grand Rapids: Zondervan, 2011.

______. *Covenant and Salvation: Union with Christ.* Louisville, KY: Westminster/John Knox Press, 2007.

______. *Introducing Covenant Theology*. Grand Rapids: Baker Books, 2009.

Hughes, Philip Edgcumbe. *A Commentary on the Epistle to the Hebrews*. Grand Rapids: Eerdmans, 1977.

Husbands, Mark A. and Daniel J. Treier, eds. *Justification: What's at Stake in the Current Debates*. Downers Grove: Inter-Varsity Press, 2004.

Ice, Thomas D. 'Covenants and Dispensations.' Last modified 2009. Accessed December 12, 2015. http://digitalcommons.liberty.edu/cgi/viewcontent.cgi?article=1002&context=pretrib_arch.

Jeon, Jeong Koo. *Covenant Theology: John Murray's and Meredith G. Kline's Response to the Historical Development of Federal Theology in Reformed Thought*. Lanham, MA: University Press of America, 2004.

______. *Covenant Theology and Justification by Faith: The Shepherd Controversy and Its Impacts*. Eugene, OR: Wipf & Stock Publishers, 2006.

Johnson, Dennis E. *Him We Proclaim: Preaching Christ from All the Scriptures*. Phillipsburg: P&R Publishing, 2007.

Johnson, Lewis S. *Discovering Romans: Spiritual Revival for the Soul*. Adapted by Mike Abendroth. Grand Rapids: Zondervan, 2014.

______. 'The Edenic Covenant.' *Covenants*. SLJ Institute, December 16, 2013. Last modified December 16, 2013. Accessed December 12, 2015. http://www.sljinstitute.net/sermons/eschatology/pages/eschatology_8.html.

______. "The Mysterious Counsel Chamber, or the Covenant of Redemption" (sermon, Believers Bible Chapel, Dallas, TX, no date), accessed January 2, 2016, http://sljinstitute.net/the-divine-purpose/the-mysterious-counsel-chamber-or-the-covenant-of-redemption/.

Johnson, William Stacy and Leith, John H. eds. *Reformed Reader: A Sourcebook in Christian Theology*. Louisville, KY: Westminster/John Knox Press, 1993.

Jones, Mark. *Antinomianism: Reformed Theology's Unwelcome Guest?* Phillipsburg: P&R Publishing, 2013.

______. *Why Heaven Kissed Earth: The Christology of the Puritan Reformed Orthodox Theologian, Thomas Goodwin (1600-1680)* (Göttingen, Germany: Vandenhoeck & Ruprecht, 2010), 124-125.

Kaiser, Walter C. "Leviticus 18:5 and Paul: Do This and You Shall Live (Eternally?)," *Journal of the Evangelical Theological Society* 15, 1 (1971): 19-28).

______. *The Promise-Plan of God: A Biblical Theology of the Old and New Testaments.* Grand Rapids: Zondervan, 2008.

Kidner, Derek. *The Message of Hosea.* Downers Grove, IL: Intervarsity Press, 1981.

Kittel, Gerhard, ed. Theological Dictionary of the New Testament Unabridged. Grand Rapids: Eerdmans, 1964.

Kline, Meredith G. *Kingdom Prologue: Genesis Foundations for a Covenantal Worldview.* Eugene, OR: Wipf and Stock Publishers, 2006.

Knight, George W. *The Pastoral Epistles: A Commentary on the Greek Text (New International Greek Testament Commentary).* 6th ed. Grand Rapids: Eerdmans, 1992.

Krapohl, Robert H, and Charles H Lippy. *The Evangelicals: A Historical, Thematic, and Biographical Guide.* Westport: Greenwood Press, 1999.

Kruse, Colin G. *The Letters of John.* Grand Rapids: Eerdmans, 2000.

Lawrence, Michael. *Biblical Theology in the Life of the Church: A Guide for Ministry.* Wheaton: Crossway, 2010.

Lee, Brian J. *Johannes Cocceius and the Exegetical Roots of Federal Theology: Reformation Developments in the Interpretation of Hebrews 7–10.* Göttingen, Germany: Vandenhoeck & Ruprecht, 2009.

Lehrer, Steve. *New Covenant Theology: Questions Answered.* n.p.: Steve Lehrer, 2006.

Leith, John H. *Assembly at Westminster: Reformed Theology in the Making.* Eugene: Wipf & Stock Publishers, 2008.

Letham, Robert. *The Work of Christ.* Downers Grove: Inter-Varsity Press, 1993.

Lightner, Robert P. *The Death Christ Died: A Biblical Case for Unlimited Atonement.* 2nd ed. Grand Rapids: Kregel Publications, 1998.

Lloyd-Jones, Martyn D. *God the Father, God the Son.* Wheaton: Crossway, 1996.

Lloyd-Jones, Sally. *The Jesus Storybook Bible Every Story Whispers His Name*. Grand Rapids: Zondervan, 2008.

Luther, Martin. *Commentary on Romans*. Grand Rapids: Kregel, 1982.

______. *Lectures On Galatians*. Saint Louis: Concordia, 1962.

MacArthur, John. *2 Corinthians (MacArthur New Testament Commentary Series)*. Chicago: Moody, 2003.

______. *2 Peter and Jude (MacArthur New Testament Commentary Series)*. Chicago: Moody, 2005.

______. *The MacArthur Study Bible*, electronic edition. Nashville: Word Pub., 1997.

______. "Submission: Heaven's Perspective on the Cross." Grace to You. September 23, 2013. Accessed February 12, 2016. http://www.gty.org/blog/B130923/heavens-perspective-on-the-cross-submission

______. "Why I Love the Church, Part 3." Grace to You. No date. Accessed February 12, 2016. http://www.gty.org/resources/articles/A352/why-i-love-the-church-part-3

MacArthur, John F. et al, *Justification by Faith Alone: Affirming the Doctrine by Which the Church and the Individual Stands or Falls.* Edited by Don Kistler. Morgan, PA: Soli Deo Gloria Publications, 1994.

Mathison, Keith A. *The Shape of Sola Scriptura.* Moscow, ID: Canon Press, 2001.

McManigal, Daniel W. *Encountering Christ in the Covenants: An Introduction to Covenant Theology*. West Linn, OR: Monergism Books, 2013.

Merritt, Jonathan. 'N.T. Wright on the Bible and Why He Won't Call Himself an Inerrantist - on Faith & Culture.' *Beliefs*. On Faith & Culture, June 2, 2014. Last modified June 2, 2014. Accessed December 12, 2015. http://jonathanmerritt.religionnews.com/2014/06/02/n-t-wright-bible-isnt-inerrantist/#sthash.GqHrAKQD.dpuf.

Miller, Samuel. *The Utility and Importance of Creeds and Confessions.* Princeton: D. A. Borrenstein, 1824.

Molnar, Paul D. *Thomas F. Torrance: Theologian of the Trinity*. Surrey: Ashgate, 1988.

Moo, Douglas J. *2 Peter, Jude*. Grand Rapids: Zondervan, 2011.

______. *The Epistle to the Romans*. Grand Rapids: Eerdmans, 1996.

Morris, Leon. *The Apostolic Preaching of the Cross*. 3rd ed. Grand Rapids: Eerdmans, 1959.

Mounce, William D. *The Analytical Lexicon to the Greek New Testament*. Grand Rapids: Zondervan, 1993.

Muller, Richard A. *Calvin and the Reformed Tradition: On the Work of Christ and the Order of Salvation*. Grand Rapids: Baker Academic.

______. *Dictionary of Latin and Greek Theological Terms: Drawn Principally from Protestant Scholastic Theology*. Grand Rapids, MI: Baker, 1985.

______. *Post-Reformation Reformed Dogmatics*. Grand Rapids: Baker, 1993.

Murray, John. *Collected Writings of John Murray, Volumes 1-4*. Carlisle, PA: Banner of Truth, 1982.

______. *Principles of Conduct: Aspects of Biblical Ethics*. Grand Rapids, MI: Eerdmans, 1957.

______. *Redemption Accomplished and Applied*. Grand Rapids: Eerdmans, 1984.

______. 'The Covenant of Grace by Dr. John Murray.' Accessed December 12, 2015. http://www.the-highway.com/Covenant_Murray.html.

______. *The Imputation of Adam's Sin*. Grand Rapids: Eerdmans, 1959.

Nichols, Stephen J. *Martin Luther: A Guided Tour of His Life and Thought*. Phillipsburg: P&R Publishing, 2003.

______. *The Reformation: How a Monk and a Mallet Changed the World*. Wheaton: Crossway, 2007.

Nichols, Stephen R. C. *Jonathan Edwards's Bible: The Relationship of the Old and New Testaments*. Eugene, OR: Pickwick Publications, 2013.

Nida, Eugene A, Rondal B Smith, and Karen A Munson. *Greek-English Lexicon of the New Testament Based on Semantic Domains Vols 1 and 2*. Edited by Johannes P Louw. New York: United Bible Societies, 1988.

O'Donnell, Laurence. 'The Holy Spirit's Role in John Owen's "Covenant of the Mediator" Formulation: A Case Study in Reformed Orthodox Formulations of the Pactum Salutis' (2015). Accessed December 12, 2015. http://www.academia.edu/3730699/The_Holy_Spirit_s_Role_in_John_Owen_s_Covenant_of_the_Mediator_Formulation_A_Case_Study_in_Reformed_Orthodox_Formulations_of_the_Pactum_Salutis.

Oliphint, K. Scott, ed. *Justified in Christ: God's Plan for Us in Justification*. Fearn, Scotland: Christian Focus, 2007.

Owen, John. *Complete Works of John Owen*. Edinburgh: Banner of Truth, 1966.

Packer, J. I. *Concise Theology: A Guide to Historic Christian Beliefs*. Carol Stream, IL: Tyndale House Publishers, 2001.

Piper, John. *Contending for Our All: Defending Truth and Treasuring Christ in the Lives of Athanasius, John Owen, and J. Gresham Machen*. Wheaton: Crossway, 2006.

______. *Counted Righteous in Christ: Should We Abandon the Imputation of Christ's Righteousness?* Wheaton: Crossway, 2002.

______. *Future Grace: The Purifying Power of the Promises of God,* revised ed. Colorado Springs: Multnomah Books, 2012.

______. "There Is No Partiality with God, Part 2." Sermon, Bethlehem Baptist Church, Minneapolis, MN, January 31, 1999. http://www.desiringgod.org/messages/there-is-no-partiality-with-god-part-2 (accessed December 12, 2015.).

Reymond, Robert L. *A New Systematic Theology of the Christian Faith: 2nd Edition - Revised and Updated.* Nashville: Thomas Nelson, 1998.

Rhodes, Jonty. *Raiding the Lost Ark: Recovering the Gospel of the Covenant King.* Nottingham: Inter-Varsity Press, 2013.

Robertson, Palmer O. *Christ of the Covenants*. 5th ed. Phillipsburg: P&R Publishing, 1981.

______. *The Current Justification Controversy*. Unicoi, TN: Trinity Foundation, 2003.

Ryrie, Charles Caldwell C. *Basic Theology*. Wheaton: Victor Books, 1986.

______. *Dispensationalism*. Chicago: Moody, 1995.

Sammons, Peter Christopher. "No Hope Without It!: The Doctrine of Active Obedience Defined and Vindicated." ThM thesis, Master's Seminary, 2013.

Shedd, William G. T. *Dogmatic Theology*. 3rd ed. Phillipsburg, NJ: P&R Publishing, 2007.

Showers, Renald E. *There Really Is a Difference!: A Comparison of Covenant and Dispensational Theology*. Bellmawr, NJ: Friends of Israel Gospel Ministry, 1990.

Schreiner, Thomas R. *1, 2 Peter, Jude*. Nashville, TN: Broadman & Holman, 2003.

______. *Faith Alone: The Doctrine of Justification*. Grand Rapids, MI: Zondervan, 2015.

______. *Paul, Apostle of God's Glory in Christ: A Pauline Theology*. Downers Grove, IL; Leicester, England: IVP Academic; Apollos, 2006.

Smith, Christian. *The Bible Made Impossible: Why Biblicism Is Not a Truly Evangelical Reading of Scripture*. Ada, MI: Brazos Press, 2011.

Snider, Andrew V. "Justification and the Active Obedience of Christ: Toward a Biblical Understanding of Imputed Righteousness." ThM thesis, Master's Seminary, 2002.

Sproul, R. C. *Faith Alone: The Evangelical Doctrine of Justification*. 3rd ed. Grand Rapids: Revell, a division of Baker Publishing Group, 1995.

Spurgeon, Charles. 'THE WONDROUS COVENANT.' Last modified 1912. Accessed December 12, 2015. http://www.spurgeongems.org/vols58-60/chs3326.pdf.

Stetzer, Ed. "Toward a Missional Convention," in *Southern Baptist Identity: An Evangelical Denomination Faces the Future,* ed. David S. Dockery. Wheaton: Crossway, 2009.

'There Is No Partiality with God, Part 2.' Desiring God, January 31, 1999. Last modified January 31, 1999. Accessed December 12, 2015. http://www.desiringgod.org/messages/there-is-no-partiality-with-god-part-2.

Trueman, Carl R. *John Owen: Reformed Catholic, Renaissance Man*. Aldershot: Ashgate Publishing, 2007.

______. *The Creedal Imperative*. Wheaton: Good News Publishers, 2012.

Turretin, Francis. *Institutes of Elenctic Theology,* vol. 1, *First Through Tenth Topics,* ed. James T. Dennison Jr, trans. George Musgrave Giger, Phillipsburg, NJ: P & R Publishing, 1992.

______. *Institutes of Elenctic Theology,* vol. 2, *First Through Tenth Topics,* ed. James T. Dennison Jr, trans. George Musgrave Giger. Phillipsburg, NJ: P & R Publishing, 1992.

______. *Justification*. Edited by James T. Dennison. Phillipsburg, NJ: P&R Publishing, 2004.

van den Brink, Gert. "Impetration and Application in John Owen's Theology," in *The Ashgate Research Companion to John Owen's Theology,* eds. Kelly M. Kapic and Mark Jones. Surrey: Ashgate, 2015.

VanDrunen, David. *Divine Covenants and Moral Order: A Biblical Theology of Natural Law*. Grand Rapids: Eerdmans, 2014.

VanDrunen, David, ed. *The Pattern of Sound Doctrine: Systematic Theology at the Westminster Seminaries: Essays in Honor of Robert B. Strimple*. Phillipsburg: P&R Publishing, 2005.

Venema, Cornelis P. *The Gospel of Free Acceptance in Christ: An Assessment of the Reformation and 'New Perspectives' on Paul.* Edinburgh: Banner of Truth, 2006.

Vlach, Michael J. "New Covenant Theology Compared with Covenantalism," *The Master's Seminary Journal* 18, 1. 2007.

Vos, Geerhardus. *Biblical Theology: Old and New Testaments*. Eugene, OR: Wipf and Stock Publishers, 2003.

______. *Redemptive History and Biblical Interpretation: The Shorter Writings of Geerhardus Vos*. Edited by Richard B. Gaffin Jr. Phillipsburg: P&R Publishing, 2001.

______. *Reformed Dogmatics: Anthropology,* ed. Richard B. Gaffin Jr. (Bellingham, WA: Lexham Press, 2012-2014), n.p. Accessed digitally on 1.19.16 via Google Books.

Walvoord, John F. *The Millennial Kingdom.* Grand Rapids, MI: Zondervan, 1959.

Waters, Guy Prentiss, and Calvin E Beisner. *The Federal Vision and Covenant Theology: A Comparative Analysis*. Phillipsburg: P&R Publishing, 2006.

Westcott, Brooke Foss. *The Epistles of St. John: The Greek Text With Notes and Essays.* London; New York: Macmillan, 1902.

White, Blake A. *What Is New Covenant Theology? An Introduction*. Frederick, MD: New Covenant Media, 2012.

Williamson, Paul R. *Sealed with an Oath: Covenant in God's Unfolding Purpose (New Studies in Biblical Theology)*. Downers Grove: Inter-Varsity Press, 2007.

Witsius, Herman. The Economy of the Covenants Between God and Man: Comprehending a Complete Body of Divinity, Volumes 1-2, 1822; repr., Kingsburg, CA: den Dulk Christian Foundation, 1990.

ABOUT THE AUTHOR

Patrick Abendroth is the Senior Pastor of Omaha Bible Church in Omaha, Nebraska where he enjoys a vibrant expository preaching ministry. He is a graduate of the University of Nebraska (B.A.), The Master's Seminary (MDiv), and Ligonier Academy (DMin). He also co-hosts a weekly theology podcast: The Pactum.

Made in United States
Orlando, FL
28 April 2023